LISTOPIA

PLANET EARTH

50 FASCINATING TOP 10 LISTS!

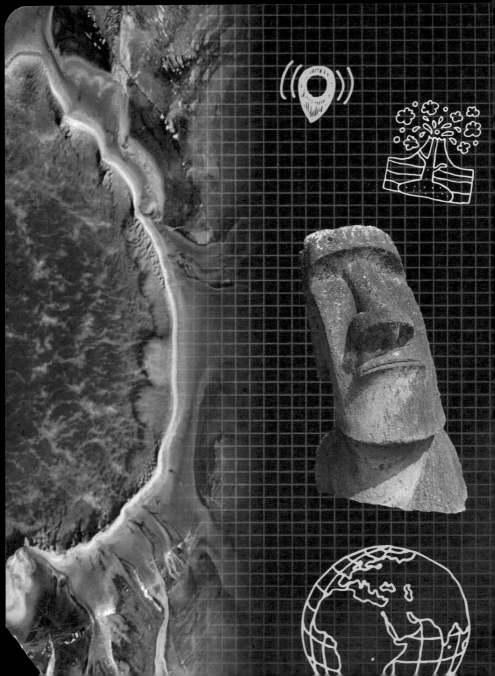

LISTOPIA

PLANET EARTH

little bee books

An imprint of Bonnier Publishing Group
853 Broadway, New York, New York 10003

Authors: James Buckley Jr., Diane Bailey
Editor: Lydia Halliday
Designer: Allen Boe
Publisher: Donna Gregory

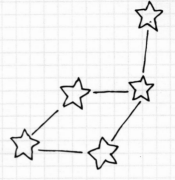

Manufactured in China 251215

First Edition 10 9 8 7 6 5 4 3 2 1

Library of Congress Cataloging-in-Publication data is
available upon request.

ISBN: 978-1-4998-0279-5

littlebeebooks.com
bonnierpublishing.com

CONTENTS

INTRODUCTION

When someone asks you what you did today, you'll list everything you did. When you talk about what you had for dinner last night, you'll list what you ate. When you don't turn your homework in, trust us . . . you'll have a list of excuses ready to go!

People naturally think of things in lists. You could say that the alphabet is a list of letters, or a dictionary is a list of words. Of course, you're on all sorts of lists, from your classroom list to your sports team roster. Lists are such a natural way of looking at the world that we decided to look at the world using lists!

In this book, you'll find hundreds of amazing facts and pieces of information about the world we all live in. Travel around the world to see beaches, mountains, waterfalls, rainforests, and more. Visit tiny countries and crowded cities.

Check out weird and wonderful things like trees (and treehouses), caves, lakes, and more. Rocket down a rollercoaster at a theme park or dance at a national festival. Discover the most amazing ocean occurrences or marvel at the world's tallest buildings.

Many of the lists are ranked; but sometimes things might change over time. Other lists aren't ranked at all; they're just great examples we thought you might like to see!

Read it through from front to back, or just open up a page at random. When you're done, check off all the items from this list that describe how you feel about this book.

MY LISTOPIA LIST

____ This book was amazing!

____ This was the best book ever!

____ I couldn't put this book down!

____ This book is a rectangle!

____ Please make more Listopia books!

MOST DANGEROUS VOLCANOES ON THE PLANET

Volcanoes are disasters waiting to happen. When they erupt, they can be among the most destructive forces on Earth. Some are more dangerous than others, mostly because they are located close to heavily populated areas. Scientists are watching these carefully . . . stay tuned! Here are 10 of the world's most threatening volcanoes.

10. MAUNA LOA
HAWAII

One of the world's most active volcanoes. Eruptions can be huge and produce fast flowing rivers of lava.

9. TAAL VOLCANO
PHILIPPINES

Taal is watched closely due to its location near the nation's capital city of Manila, home to more than 1.6 million people.

8. ULAWUN
PAPUA NEW GUINEA

A structural collapse of this volcano would cause an eruption that could devastate hundreds of square miles.

7. MT. NYIRAGONGO
DEMOCRATIC REPUBLIC OF CONGO

Nyiragongo has a large, active lava lake. The lava runs like water when the lake drains, threatening anything in its path.

6. MT. MERAPI INDONESIA

Hundreds of villages are located less than 5 miles away from this potential disaster.

5. GALERAS COLOMBIA

The city of Pasto, home to 450,000 people, is located on the eastern slope of Galeras.

4. SAKURAJIMA
JAPAN

Sakurajima is in constant activity, erupting every 4 to 24 hours. It frequently deposits ash on the nearby city of Kagoshima.

3. POPOCATÉPETL
MEXICO

One of the world's most active volcanoes, an eruption would threaten up to 9 million people who live nearby.

2. MT. VESUVIUS
ITALY

Vesuvius presents a major danger to the nearby densely populated city of Naples. Vesuvius is most famous for its eruption in 79 AD, when a huge column of ash rose high into the sky, completely destroying the Roman cities of Pompeii and Herculaneum.

1. YELLOWSTONE SUPERVOLCANO

The supervolcano in Yellowstone National Park is considered the most dangerous because of the sheer destruction it would cause if it were to erupt. An explosion would wipe out the entire western USA, killing an estimated 87,000 people instantly. The ash would affect the health of people throughout the world for years to come.

◄ OLD FAITHFUL
One of the largest geysers (hot springs that erupt at regular intervals) in Yellowstone. It can reach heights of 184 feet.

▲ **AMAZING COLORS**
An aerial view of the Grand Prismatic Spring in the Yellowstone caldera (volcanic crater) reveals beautiful colors.

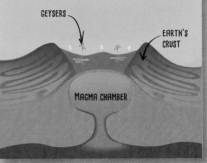

INSIDE THE CALDERA

Below Earth's surface, magma (molten rock) rises from a hotspot. Because Earth's crust is quite thick, the magma continues to build up underground in the magma chamber.

GEYSERS

EARTH'S CRUST

MAGMA CHAMBER

The yellow section shows the area that would be affected if the volcano were to erupt.

The volcano is located in Yellowstone National Park, Wyoming, USA.

HIGHEST WATERFALLS ON THE PLANET

Water, like everything else on Earth, has to obey the law. In this case, it's the law of gravity. When flowing water meets a steep cliff, the result is a waterfall. They can be truly spectacular sights. Here are the 10 highest in the world.

10. BROWNE FALLS
SOUTH ISLAND, NEW ZEALAND

This cascade plummets into the Doubtful Sound Fiord, but there is no doubting the rugged beauty of these mountains. 2,744 feet.

9. JAMES BRUCE FALLS
BRITISH COLUMBIA, CANADA

North America's tallest waterfall, though not its most beautiful. Fed by a pool high in the Canadian Rockies, this is described at some points as a "trickle." But a *falling* trickle! 2,755 feet.

8. PU'UKA'OKU FALLS
MOLOKAI, HAWAII

Located at the highest point of a coastline of Hawaiian waterfalls that spill out to the sea, we couldn't fail to include these magnificent falls. 2,756 feet.

7. SKORGA NORWAY

Next time you're driving down Highway 70 near Sunndalen, Norway, pull over for an amazing view of this waterfall. Fed by a melting glacier, it spills down an almost vertical cliff face. 2,835 feet.

6. Vinnufallet
Norway

Skorga is nice . . . Vinnufallet is nicer! This is the tallest waterfall in Europe, and it can be seen from the highway. The Vinnu Glacier is the source of the water here. 2,837 feet.

5. Yumbilla Peru

The Andes Mountains contain a number of broad, flat plateaus. At the edges are very tall cliff faces, and off those edges plunge some amazing waterfalls. This one in Peru is the second-tallest in its region but has the highest water flow. Stay tuned for more in Peru! 2,938 feet.

4. Olo'upena Falls
Molokai, Hawaii

The north shore of all the Hawaiian islands have been battered by wind and waves for thousands of years. The resulting cliffs have created a series of huge waterfalls. This is the tallest, and it is truly a spectacular sight. 2,953 feet.

3. Tres Hermanas
Peru

The rugged Andes created the site of this super-tall waterfall. It's now part of a national park so that the beauty of this area can be protected. 3,000 feet.

2. Tugela Falls
South Africa

Hikers can make their way to the top and sides of this largest African waterfall. It's the highlight of a visit to Royal Natal National Park. 3,110 feet.

1. KEREPAKUPAI MERÚ OR ANGEL FALLS VENEZUELA

Known to locals as Kerepakupai Merú, Angel Falls is the world's tallest waterfall. Like many on this list, it is a series of cascades, but it includes the longest unbroken fall of water in the world. At one point, water drops straight down a cliff face for 2,648 feet. The edges of the cliff are formed by a broad plateau of land in the northern Amazon rainforest. 3,212 feet.

WHY ANGEL?

Though the water falling here might seem to come from the heavens, the falls actually got their name from an American named Jimmy Angel. He was a pilot exploring the region from the air in 1933. After spotting the falls, he landed near the top of them. Then his plane got stuck in the thick soil, and he had to hike out—that took him 11 days!

FAMOUS PLACES OF WORSHIP

Places of worship have been built for thousands of years to allow people to gather together to worship the god or gods they believe in. A church or a temple can be as simple as a clearing in a forest or as elaborate as a golden building with enormous towers. No matter what you believe about religion, check out these wonders of both design and faith.

ST. PETER'S BASILICA
ROMAN CATHOLICISM

The world center of the Catholic faith is in Vatican City, which is actually its own very tiny country inside the city limits of Rome, Italy. The church was named after one of Jesus's apostles. Construction began in 1506 and took more than a century. Popes live in buildings near the church, which features artwork by Michelangelo, Bernini, and other legendary figures.

ANKGOR WAT
BUDDHISM

Cambodia is home to this collection of more than 100 gorgeous Buddhist temples. They were built from 800 to 1,200 years ago, mostly by Khmer people. The tallest of these temples stands at a staggering 669 feet.

DJINGUEREBER MOSQUE ISLAM

This is not the biggest or most grand mosque in the world, but it is one of the most unique. Located in Timbuktu, Mali, this is one of the largest buildings in the world made entirely of mud bricks. Local architects have constantly maintained the mosque since it was built in 1327.

Hagia Sophia
Islam

Located in Istanbul, Turkey, this massive building was once the centerpiece of the Christian church in the Eastern world, and later one of the largest mosques in the world. Built by Justinian in 537 CE, it was an Orthodox Christian Church until the Islamic Empire took over the city in 1453. The building was turned into a museum to both faiths in 1935 by the Turkish government.

Westminster Abbey
Anglican Christian

British monarchs have been presented with their crowns in this London church since the eleventh century. It has been renovated several times, but it remains the center of English religious life. Kings, poets, nobles, and others are buried within its crypts, making it a regular part of many London tourist trips. People around the world have watched several famous royal weddings take place there, too.

Western Wall
Judaism

This is not actually a Jewish temple, but part of the outside of what was once a large temple that was destroyed in 70 AD. However, its symbolic role in the Jewish religion remains large, and thousands of people go to pray there every day. It is located in Jerusalem.

Golden Temple
Sikhism

This faith is practiced by more than 30 million people, mostly in India. The full name of the Golden Temple is Sri Harimandir Sahib Amritsar, and it was completed in 1577. It has four entrances, which represent that people are welcome from any direction.

MEENAKSHI AMMAN
HINDUISM

Hindu temples are among the world's most elaborate and artistic. Tens of thousands of them are built throughout Asia. But many point to this one in Madurai, India, as one of the most beautiful, built to honor a warrior-goddess named Meenakshi.

ST. BASIL'S CATHEDRAL
RUSSIAN ORTHODOX CHRISTIANITY

Located on Moscow's Red Square, St. Basil's was completed in 1561 under the direction of Tsar Ivan the Terrible. Nine separate churches are contained in the group, many of which have the famous "onion dome" tops, decorated in bright colors.

WHAT IS A HAJJ?

All observant Muslims believe they must follow several key things which are known as the Five Pillars. The first is to believe in Allah as god and Muhammad as his prophet. The second is to pray five times a day. The third is to do acts of charity. The fourth is the celebration of the annual fast during the holy month of Ramadan. The fifth is called the Hajj, a trip to Mecca. Every Muslim who is healthy and can afford it is supposed to make at least one Hajj in their lifetime. Pilgrims—there are millions every year—must wear white, unstitched clothing. They walk in circles together around the Kaaba, praying and asking for forgiveness for sins.

MASJID AL-HARAM

This is the largest mosque in the world. Located in the city of Mecca, it is the place toward which Muslims worldwide turn while offering daily prayers. Surrounding a cube called the Kaaba, it is Islam's holiest place. When Muslim pilgrims make their once-in-a-lifetime trip to Mecca, they don white clothing and walk around the Kaaba nine times, joined by thousands of fellow Muslims. In fact, the area is so sacred that non-Muslims are not allowed into most areas of the Grand Mosque.

Though completed mostly in the sixteenth century, the site dates much further back in Islamic history. The prophet Muhammad returned to Mecca in 630 CE and established the city and the site as the centerpiece of the faith.

10 MOST POPULOUS NATIONS

"Most populous nations" means the countries that have the most people living in them. The whole world is packed with more than 7 billion people, and more are being born every day. About 100 years ago, Earth was home to less than 2 billion. This place is getting crowded!

10. JAPAN 127 MILLION

In terms of land area, Japan is the smallest nation on this top ten list, making it number one in population density. That means the most people squeezed into the least space!

9. RUSSIA 142 MILLION

Russia is the largest country in the world, but only 9th in terms of number of people. Most of its large population is in major cities in the western part of the country, especially its capital, Moscow.

8. BANGLADESH 166 MILLION

Hot, wet weather and the crowded conditions have made Bangladesh one of the poorest nations on Earth. Most people are farmers growing food only for themselves.

7. NIGERIA 177 MILLION

Nigeria is a very diverse country; it is home to more than 250 ethnic groups. The discovery of oil in the country has resulted in the industrialization of many cities.

6. PAKISTAN
196 MILLION

People have lived in Pakistan's Indus Valley for more than 5,000 years, making it one of the world's oldest sites of civilization. Muslim Pakistan used to be part of Hindu India, but the two split in 1965.

4. INDONESIA 253 MILLION

Indonesia includes more than 17,000 islands, but people live on only 6,000 of them. The main island includes the massive capital city of Jakarta.

3. UNITED STATES
318 MILLION

The USA topped the 300 million mark in 2006. However, birth rates are among the lowest ever, so the population is not increasing as fast as it was before.

5. BRAZIL
202 MILLION

Most of the people of Brazil, which is South America's largest country in size and population, live along the coasts in large cities such as Rio de Janeiro and São Paulo.

2. INDIA 1.2 BILLION

Experts say that in the next few decades, India might become the world's most populous nation. India adds more people to its population every year than any other country.

1. CHINA
1.3 BILLION

The Chinese government was so worried about the population growth of the country that it started a controversial plan. As of 1980, families were only allowed to have one child each. Families with more than one child would face fines or penalties. This did help to lower the birth rate, but it also meant that many families abandoned unwanted children, especially girls. Why girls? Because boys were seen to be more likely to earn money later to take care of their elderly parents. However, in 2015, the Chinese government decided to end this policy and allow families to have two children.

China's Biggest Cities

Here's a list of the five Chinese cities with the largest populations:

	City	Population (2015 est.)
	1. Shanghai	23 million
	2. Beijing	18 million
	3. Guangzhou	12.4 million
	4. Shenzhen	12.3 million
	5. Chongqing	11 million

Most AMAZING TYPES OF TREES

They are the tallest living things on Earth, and they are also amazingly diverse. Trees help us to breathe. It's true! The vast forests of the world are part of a system that removes carbon dioxide from the atmosphere. The plants then give out oxygen that we need to breathe. Here's a list of some incredible and amazing species of individual trees from around the world.

Montezuma Cypress

Located on the grounds of a church in Santa Maria del Tule, Mexico, this massive cypress is actually protected by international law. Scientists know that it is one of the largest trees in the world, measuring 29.5 feet across. They are not sure, however, how old it is!

Giant Redwoods and Sequoias

Growing only on the western mountains and coastal lands of the USA, these related species are the tallest tree species in the world. Redwoods can be taller, topping more than 375 feet. Sequoias are almost as tall, but are wider. A protected sequoia called General Sherman is the largest living tree on the planet!

Bonsai

While redwoods reach for the sky, bonsai reach for the heart. Bonsai is not the name of a tree, but the name of a tree-shaping art that turns living trees into tiny sculptures. Artists and gardeners carefully clip firs, pines, yew trees, and dozens of other species to form mysterious and flowing shapes.

Banyan Trees

So familiar in India, they are considered the country's national tree. Banyans look like more than one tree at once. The trunks tangle together to form canopies that can stretch hundreds of feet across. Banyans are actually a member of the fig tree family.

Bristlecone Pine

This species of tree might be the oldest living thing on Earth. Bristlecone grow only on high, windswept mountains. The Great Basin National Park in Nevada, USA, is home to one tree, known as Methuselah, that is more than 4,800 years old. These trees grow very slowly, which helps them to have long lives.

Dragonblood Trees

They stand like opened umbrellas on the plains of Africa. They get their name from what is inside, however. When cut, the trees "bleed" a thick, red resin that has been used as a dye for more than 2,000 years.

Rainbow Eucalyptus

Some flowering trees produce amazing colors, but this species of tall tree has color in its bark. Native to the Philippines, rainbow eucalyptus can grow to more than 200 feet tall. Their bark can be striped with red, orange, and green patches.

Bodhi Tree

Bodhis are a type of fig that grows across southeast Asia. One particular bodhi tree, however, became world famous. Located in India and called Dharma Data, it was said that as the Buddha sat under this tree, he finally gained enlightenment. That particular tree is not there, but Buddhists are still inspired by bodhi trees.

THE WEIRDEST TREES IN THE WORLD

Baobab trees look very strange. Few plants on Earth are more unusual than these tall, bare, puffy-topped trees. There are actually nine different types of baobab tree, and some of them have pretty special adaptations for their habitats.

The baobabs of Madagascar are the most famous type of this tree. They are bare for almost their entire height before popping out leafy branches at the top. Their small home is a popular place for people to visit and snap pictures.

An African species is known as the dead-rat tree, as people thought that the hanging fruit looked like dead rodents. They are also sometimes called monkey-bread trees, as monkeys sometimes eat the squishy fruit from this type of tree.

Tree of Life

Talk about lonely. The Tree of Life sits in the middle of a vast desert in the Middle Eastern country of Bahrain. It's a mesquite tree that is about 30 feet tall, but its location makes it amazing. It is the only thing of any size growing for more than a mile in any direction. It is so rare and unique that the United Nations includes it on a list of protected natural sites.

▶ Inside a Baobab

In South Africa, one baobab tree is so big that people can stay inside it. A room and a tiny restaurant were built in and around the tree, located in a town called Modjadjiskloof.

Most POPULAR COUNTRIES FOR TOURISTS TO VISIT

Want to take a vacation? You're not alone! According to the travel industry, people spend more than $2.2 trillion while traveling. That's a lot of train tickets, museum passes, and hotel rooms! And people often choose the same places to visit. Here are the places that attracted the most visitors in 2014.

10. MEXICO
24.2 MILLION
Combine exotic beaches on both the Pacific Ocean and the Gulf of Mexico, mysterious rainforests, and the culture of Mexico City, and you've got a world-class destination.

9. RUSSIA
29.8 MILLION
The world's largest country has plenty of things for visitors to see, from Black Sea resorts to the famous onion domes in Moscow, and from the frosty north to the exotic steppes.

8. UNITED KINGDOM
32.6 MILLION
The many sights and sounds of London are the main attraction, but visitors also head to the countryside. Beautiful farmland and rolling hills make this a hiker's paradise.

7. GERMANY 33 MILLION
European visitors and people from the USA make up the bulk of tourists in Germany. Cities like Berlin and Munich are part of most people's tours.

6. Turkey
39.8 million

In Istanbul, Asia and Europe meet in a place that is thousands of years old. People come to see the history, but they also discover a very modern place to explore.

5. Italy
48.6 million

Is it just the food? Well, that certainly helps, but Italy's many attractions include busy cities and beautiful countrysides.

4. China
55.6 million

Most tourists spend their time in the capital of Beijing. There they explore the ancient Forbidden City, but they can also take a short trip to see the Great Wall of China.

3. Spain
65 million

For many people in Europe, the warm cities of Spain are the perfect summer retreat. Beaches along the Mediterranean fill up with sun-lovers.

2. United States
74.8 million

Tourists arrive in the USA every year from every nation. The diversity of the landscape is a big attraction, along with the many things to see and do in cities like New York and Los Angeles.

Once You Get Here

Here are the 10 most popular tourist sites in the USA:

1. Times Square, New York City
2. Central Park, New York City
3. Union Station, Washington, D.C.
4. Las Vegas Strip, Nevada
5. Grand Central Terminal, New York City
6. Disneyworld, Orlando, Florida
7. Disneyland, Anaheim, California
8. Golden Gate Bridge, San Francisco
9. Fanueil Hall Marketplace, Boston
10. Golden Gate Park, San Francisco

1. FRANCE
83.7 MILLION

Bonjour, tout le monde! That means "Hello, everybody!" in French. For most of the 2000s, France has been at or near the top of this list. Why is it so popular? Its central location in Europe helps, as people from around the continent have just a short journey to reach Paris or the southern beaches. Americans have loved coming to France for more than a century, drawn by the historic sites, the amazing food, and a certain *je ne sais quoi* (which means "I don't know what!"). France brings out a feeling in people that is hard to describe. People visit looking to experience that feeling in person. They walk the streets of Paris and imagine living there. They hike a meadow in the south of France and breathe in the fresh air. They lie on the sandy beaches of the Mediterranean and let the sun push winter away. *La belle France* means "beautiful France." More than 80 million tourists each year seem to agree.

Top Five Places in Paris

If you're heading to Paris, expect these famous sights to be the most crowded:

▲ Pompidou Center

▲ Notre Dame

▲ Louvre Museum

▲ Eiffel Tower

► Sacré-Coeur

Most Popular
Theme Parks

People around the world love to visit theme parks for their rides, shows, and atmosphere. From Disneyland to Universal Studios and more, the parks transport people to magical places. Visitors can soar with Harry Potter, dive with dolphins, travel to the stars with Luke Skywalker, or just pretend they're on Main Street, USA. Two companies dominate theme parks around the world—Disney and Universal. But which are the most popular? You can find out here . . . and you don't even have to buy a ticket!

10. Disney's California Adventure
Anaheim, California

This is the newest park on this list, and it opened in 2001. It is right next door to Disneyland, which means that many tourists plan two or three days to make it through both places.

9. Disneyland Paris
Paris, France

Though it did not start out well, this French version of Mickey's home has jumped into the top ten. Built 20 miles outside of Paris, it features hotels and a separate park about movies.

8. Disney's Hollywood Studios
Orlando, Florida

This is one of four Disney parks all located near each other in Florida, making the Orlando area a one-stop shop for theme park fans. The Studios feature the Tower of Terror thrill ride.

7. DISNEY'S ANIMAL KINGDOM ORLANDO, FLORIDA

Most of the Disney parks on this list focus on imaginary people and creatures. At its Animal Kingdom park in Florida, the focus is on animals that are very real—lions, tigers, elephants, rhinos, and more. Guests can take a ride through the park's vast fields to see the animals in habitats much like those they inhabit in the wild. The Wild Africa Trek is on walkways above the animals, so you can peer down on hippos as they splash around! On the Kilimanjaro safari, ride in an open car just feet away from ostriches, giraffes, lions, and more. Not every theme park is based on the make-believe. Some, like this one, can be great learning experiences, too.

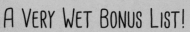

A Very Wet Bonus List!

At some theme parks such as Seaworld, you can see animals splash around. But what about people? Waterparks have become very popular around the world. Here are the ones at which the most people got soaking wet!

CHIMELONG WATERPARK, GUANGZHOU, CHINA
TYPHOON LAGOON AT DISNEY WORLD, ORLANDO, FLORIDA
BLIZZARD BEACH AT DISNEY WORLD, ORLANDO, FLORIDA
THERMAS DOS LARANJAIS, OLIMPIA, BRAZIL
OCEAN WORLD, GANGWON-DO, SOUTH KOREA

6. EPCOT ORLANDO, FLORIDA

Walt Disney loved the future and loved to think about what we could achieve if we put our minds to it. He came up with the name of this park, which was designed to showcase new ideas and new technologies. EPCOT stands for Experimental Prototype Community of Tomorrow. A prototype is an example of a new idea. For Disney, EPCOT was an example of the future of theme parks. Today, it includes exhibitions of inventions from around the world and a space-themed thrill ride.

5. UNIVERSAL STUDIOS Japan

The original Universal Studios theme park is in Burbank, California, but its Japanese cousin now attracts way more visitors. Attractions include roller coasters, stunt shows, and rides connected to movies created by Universal.

4. TOKYO DISNEYSEA Japan

Travel around the world without leaving Japan at this unique park. Its seven "lands" are all connected to famous sea and water stories, from Captain Nemo's Mysterious Island to the Mississippi River tales of Mark Twain to Mermaid Lagoon.

3. DISNEYLAND Anaheim, California

Opened in 1955, this is the oldest park on the list, but still one of the most popular. All the other Disney resorts and parks look to this original one for inspiration. Centered on Sleeping Beauty's castle, Disneyland now includes eight "lands," including Main Street USA, Fantasyland, and Toontown.

2. TOKYO DISNEYLAND Japan

This far-off cousin of California's Disneyland now gets more visitors than the original park. In 2014, more than 17 million people poured through the gates in search of fantasy, magic, and lots of souvenirs!

1. MAGIC KINGDOM AT WALT DISNEY WORLD
Lake Buena Vista, Florida

Walt Disney World reigns atop this list. With more than 52,000 people visiting it every single day of the year, that's like an entire football stadium entering the park every morning!

LONGEST BRIDGES

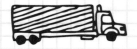

Bridges can be as simple as a log dropped across a small stream or as complicated as long structures that span part of a sea. For this list, we chose to include bridges over water. There are some long bridges above land that might have qualified, but where they stop being roads and start being bridges can be tricky to define. So here we have the longest bridges over water, enjoy the view!

10. VASCO DE GAMA BRIDGE
PORTUGAL, 10.7 MILES

The capital city of Lisbon is split by the huge mouth of the Tagus River. To connect the two parts of the city, this bridge opened in 1998. It is so long that engineers had to compensate for how Earth curves while building it!

9. JINTANG BRIDGE
CHINA, 16.4 MILES

A group of large islands, including the largest, Zhousan, lies off the east-central coast of China. This mighty bridge is the longest in a series that connects the islands to the mainland.

8. CHESAPEAKE BAY BRIDGE—TUNNEL
VIRGINIA, USA, 17.6 MILES

The eastern part of Maryland is split by the famous Chesapeake Bay. This bridge travels across that body of water to connect the two parts of Maryland and also allows you to reach Delaware a bit farther on.

7. Atchafalaya Basin Bridge
Louisiana, USA, 18.2 miles

While most bridges over water soar high above a river or a lake, this roadway is only a few feet above a vast swamp. Drivers can look down at the dark green water and the many plants that grow there.

5. Runyang Bridge
China, 22.1 miles

6. Donghai Bridge
China, 20.2 miles

The port of the large city of Shanghai is on Yangshan Island. Until this bridge opened in 2008, the only way to reach the port was by ship. The bridge now takes drivers across the East China Sea between city and port.

Spanning the Yangtze River, near the major city of Nanjing, this bridge is one of two that travel between Yangzhou to the north and Zhenjiang to the south. They are part of a major north–south route in eastern China.

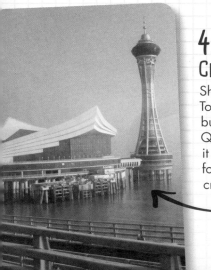

4. Hangzhou Bay Bridge
China, 22.4 miles

Shanghai is one of the world's largest cities. To reach its southern suburbs, this bridge was built in 2005 across Hangzhou Bay where the Qiantang River has its mouth. It is so long that it has an island near the middle with services for travelers. Some people call it the longest cross-ocean bridge in the world.

3. Manchac Bridge
Louisiana, USA, 22.8 miles

Leaving New Orleans from the south and heading west, you either need this bridge or a boat! The large Manchac swamp lies over most of the land to the city's southwest, but this bridge provides safe passage.

2. Lake Ponchartrain Causeway Bridge
Louisiana, USA, 23.9 miles

So is a causeway a bridge? That's a point some experts debate. Officially, this super-long structure is called a causeway as it spans Lake Ponchartrain near New Orleans. But it is a single structure that goes over water, so we're going to leave it on this list thanks to its worldwide fame.

Stay Tuned!

Look for this list to change. Construction is underway on a bridge that will connect the Chinese islands of Hong Kong and Macau and the city of Zhuhai. The bridge is planned to span 18.4 miles. Since Hong Kong and Macau have some separate government functions from China, there will also be a border crossing built into the bridge.

▶ Famous Bridges

Several of the world's most famous bridges aren't on the list of longest, but they're worth taking a look at.

1. The Golden Gate Bridge is painted bright orange, spans the entry into San Francisco Bay, and connects the city to Marin County in the north.

2. The Brooklyn Bridge in New York is made from stone and opened in 1883. It was the longest suspension bridge in the world at that time, more than a mile long.

3. Tower Bridge is one of London's most famous landmarks. Its center section can be raised and lowered to let ships pass through underneath.

1. QINGDAO HAIWAN BRIDGE CHINA, 26.4 MILES

The bridge on Lake Ponchartrain lost its top spot in 2011, when this engineering marvel opened for traffic. Crossing Jiaozhou Bay in northeast China, the Qingdao set a new world record for length. How long is it? If they got all the cars out of the way and ran a race there . . . it would be as long as a marathon! Building began from each side in 2007. Engineers had to calculate where the two sides would meet. If they were wrong by just a few inches, it would have been a disaster. Tens of thousands of cars make the long drive every day to reach the busy city of Qingdao.

LONGEST TUNNELS:
CAN YOU DIG IT?

The tunnels on this list were nearly all built to help cars get through large mountains instead of having to build a tricky road up and over the mountains. Digging and building tunnels is hard and dangerous work. Rock and dirt have to be dug out and blasted away. As the tunnel is dug, the walls have to be built to make sure it doesn't all come crashing down. Engineers have to be very careful in designing tunnels to withstand the enormous pressure of the mountain on top! These tunnels are so long that you definitely can't play the "hold-your-breath-in-a-tunnel" game!

10. BAOJIASHAN
CHINA, 7 MILES

Xian is a major city in central China, near the Qinling mountains. To reach a neighboring city to the south, Ankang, drivers on the G30 expressway go through this tunnel, the third longest in China.

9. GUDVANGEN
NORWAY, 7.1 MILES

Want to get from Bergen to Oslo in time for the ferry? Then you'll spend about 20 minutes in this two-lane tunnel through the Aurland region of Norway.

8. MONT BLANC
FRANCE TO ITALY, 7.2 MILES

At 15,781 feet, Mont Blanc is the highest mountain on the continent of Europe. Far below is this busy tunnel connecting Italy and France. Following a terrible vehicle fire in 1999, new safety and fire prevention systems were put in place in the Mont Blanc tunnel.

7. Majishan Tunnel
China, 7.6 miles

Located almost in the very center of China, this four-lane tunnel keeps traffic flowing on a busy east-west highway.

5. Hsuehshan Tunnel
Taiwan, 8 miles

This long stretch of tunnel on the island of Taiwan has computer-controlled lights and video to help control traffic and speeds, making this 8-mile trip quick and safe.

4. Arlberg
Austria, 8.7 miles

Getting out of a tunnel in an emergency is part of every tunnel plan. This tunnel through the Austrian Alps goes one step further, creating more than 60 ways for people to get out in case of trouble.

6. Frejus
France to Italy, 8 miles

Two tunnels connect France and Italy through the Italian Alps. One lets traffic flow, with border crossings at each end. The other is dedicated to rescue and safety . . . just in case!

3. St. Gotthard Tunnel Switzerland, 10.5 miles

How busy is this tunnel connecting Switzerland with the road south to Italy? There is so much traffic that a second, parallel tunnel is in the planning stages. Traffic jams often pack this tunnel with cars for hours.

2. Qinling Zhongnanshan Tunnel
China, 11.2 miles

This is the longest twin-tube tunnel in the world. That means four lanes of traffic can travel through. Along the way, drivers are entertained by pictures of clouds and plants projected onto the walls!

1. LAERDAL TUNNEL
NORWAY, 15.2 MILES

Norwegians are good at making tunnels! Dozens of them are used to help people get around this mountainous country. The Laerdal Tunnel connects Aurland and the beautiful Laerdal Valley in north-central Norway. Workers had to dig for five years to build this two-lane road that runs through almost solid rock. They used a massive tunnel-boring machine that chews up rock and stone, and tunneled from both ends using satellites to make sure each end was going in the right direction. Lasers were also used in the tunnels to create perfectly straight lines, too. The tunnel stretches so far that a separate tunnel was dug near its middle. That way if the tunnel was blocked near one end or an accident closed lanes, rescue workers could still get inside.

◀ **COMING SOON!**
Another tunnel may have jumped onto this list by the time you read about it. The Mount Ovit Tunnel is planned to run through 9.1 miles of rugged mountains in northeastern Turkey. Work started in 2012. The tunnel was due to be ready to open in either 2015 or 2016.

Lærdals-tunnelen

•24,5 km

Booorrrrring!

Tunnels have to be bored, of course, but the rides in them don't have to be boring (get it?). When building Laerdal, engineers worked with scientists to design curves and slopes so that drivers would not be lulled to sleep by a long, straight drive. The use of special lighting also helps to change the "scenery" a bit. It can take more than 30 minutes to get through the tunnel, so the aim was to make sure everyone made it through safely!

WORLD'S COLDEST PLACES!

Believe it or not, people live for months at a time in cold weather that would probably send most of us diving under the blankets. At spots in high mountains and in high latitudes (that is, closer to the north and south poles), the lack of sunlight and thin air creates perfect conditions for very cold weather. Listed here are the lowest air temperatures ever recorded on Earth. If you plan to visit, make sure you pack your earmuffs!

KITTILÄ FINLAND, 1999 (MINUS 60.7°F)

To reach Kittilä, you have to cross the Arctic Circle and keep going north. Though a popular ski resort as well as a mining center, this Finnish town can also be one of the coldest spots on Earth.

Just because the climate of an area is generally warm doesn't mean it can't have cold records. Check out these cold-weather trivia tidbits:

COLDEST IN AFRICA: IFRANE, MOROCCO, 1935 -12°F (1935)

COLDEST IN SOUTH AMERICA: SAN JUAN PROVINCE, ARGENTINA -38°F (1972)

SNOW ON THE EQUATOR! CAYAMBE MOUNTAINS, PART OF THE ANDES IN ECUADOR

ROGERS PASS MONTANA, USA, 1954 (MINUS 70.6°F)

Snowbound most of the winter, this location high in the Rocky Mountains has held the continental USA record for more than 50 years! What about the lowest annual average temperature? For the United States, the winner is Barrow, Alaska, which has averaged about 11.7°F over the past 30 years.

SNAG YUKON, CANADA, 1947 (MINUS 83°F)

Show some skin in weather this cold and it will freeze in less than 3 minutes! A Siberian air mass created this Canadian all-time record, which is saying something, since Canada also has recorded dozens of temperatures of more than 50 degrees below zero Fahrenheit.

NORTH ICE STATION GREENLAND, 1954 (MINUS 87°F)

For two years, British researchers lived on the snowy, rocky, wind-swept heights of this station on Greenland. While they were there, instruments at the station recorded the lowest temperature ever in North America. Brrrr!

OYMYAKON RUSSIA, 1933 (MINUS 89.9°F)

Want to talk about a great tourist town? Then you probably won't be talking about this far-off outpost of civilization in Siberia, Russia. Oymyakon is the coldest place on Earth in which people live year-round. How cold is it? To prevent cars from freezing, most people leave the engines running all day and night. If someone dies, they have to burn the ground to thaw it out before digging a grave. A regular treat? Frozen meat, since it can be more expensive to heat up than to buy the meat. And did we mention that it's dark 21 hours a day for months at a time during winter? Average winter temperatures are around -50°F. A photographer reported that he had to hold his breath while shooting, otherwise his breath cloud would fog the lens!

A NEW LOW:
A SPOT ON THE EAST ANTARCTIC PLATEAU, 2010 (−135.8°F)

In 2010, scientists used new satellite and ground-based radar instruments to find the coldest spot on Earth. The previous record holder at the Vostok Research Station (Antarctica) was not nearly as high above sea level as this spot on the east Antarctic Plateau. No one was here in person for the measurement . . . no one could have likely survived outside to read a thermometer anyway! No life can exist—that we know of—at temperatures this low.

THE OLD LOW: VOSTOK STATION, ANTARCTICA, 1983 (−128.5°F)

Scientists were actually inside the station to measure the outside temperature for this second-coldest day. Research stations like this one are not all staffed year-round. For one thing, no rescue airplanes or ships could reach them in case of emergency for months at a time. In fact, anyone who volunteers to do research in this isolated spot has to have already had their appendix and wisdom teeth removed. This is to avoid at least those two emergencies causing problems for hard-to-reach outposts. The windchill here was once recorded at as low as −191°F in 2005!

COLD SNAP!

When temperatures plunge to well below freezing, bad things can happen to the human body. In some places, the air can be too cold to breathe. Some scientists working in the Antarctic breathe through snorkels that pass air through tubes next to their body. That way the air is heated enough to breathe.

The body also wants to keep its most important parts warm, so in extreme cold, blood rushes from the limbs to the head and trunk. With less blood in the fingers and toes, the body has less protection from the cold. Frostbite can literally kill fingers, toes, feet, and more. What about our eyeballs? Actually, they can't really freeze since they're in your head, which the body wants to keep warm. Tears are also salty, so that keeps them from freezing. But your nose can freeze! Best option when you're cold? Get indoors quickly!

Extreme Heat!

Measuring air temperature is not as easy as it sounds. Over time, the instruments to measure heat have become better and better. Today, we can even use satellites. Comparing heat records from long ago to today can just create lots of disagreement among scientists and weather-watchers. So rather than get into the debates about the ten hottest places of all time, here is a list of recognized heat extremes, according to the World Meteorological Organization.

Hottest Place Ever!

On a lovely summer day in July of 1913, the temperature in Death Valley, California, reached 134°F, now recognized as the highest air temperature ever recorded.

World's Hottest Place With People

Bangkok wins the title for the world's hottest city; however, it is the villages in Dallol, Ethiopia, that are the world's hottest inhabited places. Annual temperatures average 94°F! That's just the average! And don't forget the humidity!

HIGHEST SURFACE TEMPERATURE EVER

Using satellites, scientists can now search the globe for high temperatures. They are looking for how hot the ground is, not how hot the air is. Since the ground can retain heat over time, it can get much hotter than the air above it. In 2004, an area of the Dasht-e Lut desert in Iran set off alarms by reaching 158°F, according to satellite readings. That was the highest (non-volcano-related) temperature ever to be recorded on Earth.

HOTTEST SOUTHERN HEMISPHERE TEMPERATURE

Why should the northern hemisphere (see "Death Valley") have all the fun? In February 1960, the temperature reached 123°F in Oodnadatta, Australia. Say "G'day" to air conditioning!

GRAVEL ROAD

MORE HOT SPOTS

Want more year-round hot places? This list includes the hottest countries in the world, measured by how many high-temperature readings are recorded each year. There are cold places in most of these countries, but these are annual highs.

1. Libya (131°F)
2. Saudi Arabia (129°F)
3. Iraq (122°F)
4. Algeria (122°F)
5. Iran (113°F)

HOTTEST YEAR EVER!

This is not a record that we wanted to set, but 2014 was the hottest year of all time. The National Oceanic and Atmospheric Administration reported temperatures that were 1.24°F above average. It might not seem like much, but that was the highest above average they had ever measured since 1880! This continues an alarming trend. The Earth is clearly getting warmer and warmer. World air temperatures have been going up steadily for many years. Why is this a problem? The air and water on Earth are in a delicate balance, along with all the life on the planet. When the temperature of the air and water rise, it can damage that balance. Scientists agree that this rise is nearly all caused by human beings—by using fossil fuels, we pump gases into the air that trap heat on Earth. The more we do this, the more the temperature goes up. We are now all looking at things we can do to reduce this sort of damage to our planet in the future.

TOP 10 WARMEST YEARS SINCE 1880

2014	2013	2009
2010	2003	2007
2005	2002	
1998	2006	

What do all of these have in common? All but one happened in the 2000s. That means nearly ever year in this century has been hotter than almost every year in the last century. If this continues, it will have a bad effect on our planet.

▶ TOO THICK TO BREATHE

One of the results of using fossil fuels is smog. This is smoke combined with natural fog. In some cities, the smog gets so bad that people have to wear masks as they walk around to keep gunk from getting in their lungs. The city of Shanghai, China, is often at the top the list of the world's smoggiest places. Cities in Iran, India, Egypt, Mexico, Russia, and Pakistan are also on the list.

Deepest Caves

Stack two of the tallest buildings in the world on top of each other, and then flip them upside down into a big hole in the ground. The top of this tower would only barely reach the limit of the tenth-deepest cave. The world beneath the surface of the Earth is dotted with amazing empty places. From our earliest days on the planet, people have explored caves. At first, they were places to live. Today, they are scientific wonders. Using high-tech gear and the courage to explore tiny, cramped, dark, tight spaces, cave explorers, called spelunkers, have reached down into Earth to discover these record-breaking caves.

10. Cehi SLOVENIA, 4,928 FEET

Italian spelunkers have mapped out much of this system of caves, which are on the border between Italy and Slovenia.

9. Sima de la Cornisa SPAIN, 4,944 FEET

As deep as this cave is, the Spanish experts who mapped it think it could go much farther. They stopped when they reached what they called a "bottomless pit."

8. Shakta Vjacheslav Patjukhina GEORGIA, 4,948 FEET

A massif is a group of mountains. In a massif in the central Asian country of Georgia, there are more than 400 caves. This one is the deepest so far, but experts think others might be even deeper.

7. TORCA DEL CERRO DEL CUEVON SPAIN, 5,213 FEET

Caving is not just a question of hiking downhill. Cavers need the skills of mountaineers in reverse. Of course, they have to climb back out, too. This Spanish cave has some tight stretches that call for the limits of the cavers' expertise.

6. RESEAU JEAN BERNARD
FRANCE, 5,256 FEET

The French Alps in the south of France are honeycombed with deep caves. Until 1980, when it was overtaken by others, the Reseau Jean Bernard was the deepest explored cave in the world.

5. VOGELSHACHT AND THE LAMPRECHTSOFEN
AUSTRIA, 5,354 FEET

Two very deep caves in Austria were discovered to be connected in one very deep cave! Near the resort town of Salzburg, Polish explorers found that this connection took them a mile deep underground for the first time.

4. GOUFFRE MIROLDAEN
FRANCE, 5,685 FEET

Another two-cave connection took cavers past a milestone. When cavers connected Gouffre Mirolda with the Lucien Coudlier they found that they could descend past 0.6 miles for the first time.

3. Illuzia-Snezhnaja Mexhonnogo
Georgia, 5,748 Feet

The French cave was overtaken in 2007 when Russian explorer Aleksey Shelepin led a team into the Georgian mountains to map out this massive cave. But pretty soon, another cave knocked even this one off the top spot.

Measuring the Deep

How do cavers know how far down they have gone? Do they bring a long string and measure it later? No, not really. Like pilots or parachutists, they use a handheld device called an altimeter. Instead of measuring how high they fly, the altimeter measures how deep they go.

2. Sarma Georgia, 6,004 Feet

Another Georgian cave, Sarma includes some massive chambers as well as long underground cliff faces. Cavers use long ropes to rappel down the interior walls. Stay tuned, as cavers believe this one might go much, much deeper!

Cave Glossary
Want to talk like a spelunker? Here is some of the lingo used underground.

ABSEIL: LOWER YOURSELF DOWN A CLIFF WITH A ROPE

CHIMNEY: A NARROW PASSAGE UPWARD BETWEEN PARALLEL FACES OF ROCK

COBBLE: A ROCK ABOUT THE SIZE OF A SOFTBALL

DEAD CAVE: A CAVE WITHOUT ANY SIGN OF WATER

DUCK-UNDER: A PASSAGE THAT IS FILLED WITH WATER

FLATTENER: A PASSAGE SO SMALL THAT A CAVER MUST CRAWL THROUGH IT ON THEIR STOMACH

GROT-HOLE: A TINY CAVE TOO TIGHT FOR A HUMAN

MOONMILK: SQUISHY CALCIUM DEPOSITS

SCROGGIN: THE CAVERS' NAME FOR A TRAIL MIX-LIKE SNACK

TROG: NICKNAME FOR A CAVER

▶ Cave Painting
How do we know people used caves long ago? They left evidence behind. People have discovered paintings on cave walls in Indonesia that scientists say are more than 40,000 years old. Other cave painting sites almost as old can be found in Australia, France, and Spain. The Indonesian paintings were only found in 2014 and were about 3,000 years older than the European ones, adding even more millennia to the history of humans on the planet.

1. KRUBERA-VORONJA CAVE
GEORGIA, 7,188 FEET

Exploring very deep caves is like climbing a mountain backward. Cavers knew that much more cave existed deep inside Krubera-Voronja. By 2001, they had reached 5,610 feet below the surface, which was then a world record. But they could see it went farther; it was just a matter of gathering the right equipment. In 2012, a team pulled together tons of gear and food and set out to break a record. They spent more than a month underground, making camps, cooking over fires, and sleeping on the warm rock. At times, they had to make scuba dives into underground pools to find out what was on the other side and to see if people could safely make it there and back. Two cavers bravely squeezed through a tube the length of a football field to find the

way down. A few weeks later, another team followed that path to the first cave deeper than 1.2 miles, setting a new record. But guess what? Cavers everywhere believe that deeper paths into Earth remain unexplored.

AMAZING STATUES AND PUBLIC ARTWORKS

It's a no-brainer to go to a museum to see paintings and statues, but there are some other pretty amazing works of art that can be seen just on a casual walk. Some are funny, some are confusing, but they're all very interesting.

METALMORPHOSIS
CHARLOTTE, NC, USA

This fountain sculpture really turns heads. Tiers of mirrored metal rotate around an axis and occasionally line up to make a human head.

THE HEADINGTON SHARK OXFORD, ENGLAND

A creative homeowner surprised his neighbors by having an enormous shark statue stuck into the roof of his house!

WATER IS LIFE
DRATCHEN, THE NETHERLANDS

Artist Henk Hofstra used 1,000 gallons of blue paint to create his "urban river," painted along a 0.62-mile strip on the street.

SPACE COW
STOCKHOLM, SWEDEN

This cow is moo-ving up—*way* up! An enormous sculpture of a cow "floats" above a street in Stockholm.

THE HAND OF THE DESERT
ATACAMA DESERT, CHILE

Five fingers stretch 36 feet high in artist Mario Irarrazabal's sculpture of a half-buried hand. Let's not even think about what's pulling that hand *down*.

Big Pencil
Aarhus, Denmark

Painted by Italian artist Blu, this mural makes you wonder if the artists is trying to make a point!

Maman
London, England

If you're scared of spiders, you might want to steer clear of this sculpture—it's 33 feet wide and 30 feet tall.

The Road of Freedom
Vilnius, Lithuania

This piece of art commemorates an important act that happened in 1989. That's when two million people joined hands in a human chain across the Baltic states of Estonia, Latvia, and Lithuania, to show they wanted independence from the Soviet Union.

The Kelpies
Falkirk, Scotland

In Scottish mythology, the kelpie is a shape-shifting water horse with the strength of 10 horses. These 98-foot kelpies must be super-strong!

STATUE OF LIBERTY

The Statue of Liberty may be the most famous statue in the entire world. Even if she is not the tallest, most impressive, or even most unusual, Lady Liberty is a global symbol of America's freedom and independence. Perched on Liberty Island in New York Harbor, the 151-foot statue was a gift from France to the USA in the late 1880s. Immigrants who came to the USA in the late 1800s and early 1900s often came through the nearby Ellis Island. When they saw the Statue of Liberty across the harbor, they knew they were almost there. Today, more than three million tourists visit the statue each year.

▶ GET HER DONE!

Although France gave the USA the statue itself, Americans were in charge of building the pedestal on which she stands. When money ran short, an influential newspaper publisher, Joseph Pulitzer, started a fundraising drive. More than 120,000 people donated—most of them less than a dollar a piece.

THE LITTLE LADIES

There are several smaller versions of the Statue of Liberty all over the world. Paris, France has three. There's one in Germany and another in Norway. There's also one in the little town of Paragould, Arkansas, USA. Denmark even has one that is built from Legos!

LONGEST GLACIERS

Covering large chunks of the polar regions, glaciers are massive sheets of moving ice. Tens of thousands of years of snow have packed down into very thick ice. That ice lies on top of land far beneath. The sheets of ice move due to gravity, sliding slowly along the land until they reach the sea or another ice shelf connected to land. Glaciers and the icy land of the poles are important to the environment, since they contain a large percentage of the world's freshwater. They also reveal secrets of the past, teaching scientists about how humans have affected the planet. Climate change has greatly affected glaciers and polar ice in recent decades. Scientists are watching them both closely for signs of trouble.

10. RECOVERY
ANTARCTICA, 62 MILES LONG

At more than 40 miles wide, this is one of the widest glaciers, too. Like many Antarctic glaciers, it drains billions of gallons of water into the ocean as it moves ever-so-slowly across the land.

9. DENMAN GLACIER
ANTARCTICA, 70 MILES LONG

In the early part of the twentieth century, several expeditions headed to the poles, trying to be the first to reach either the North or South Pole, or just to see what humans could do in the icy conditions. This glacier was named by an Australian expedition for the Governor-General of that nation.

8. SLESSOR GLACIER
ANTARCTICA, 75 MILES LONG

Located near the coast of Antarctica opposite the tip of South America, this glacier hugs the Shackleton Range. That mountain area was named for British explorer Ernest Shackleton. In 1916, Shackleton completed a two-year odyssey aiming for the South Pole. Stuck in the ice, his ship broke apart. Somehow, he led his 27 men for more than a year at the bottom of the world, finally taking a small boat across terrible seas to find help. All survived.

7. HUBBARD GLACIER ALASKA, 76 MILES LONG

Most glaciers on this list are far from easy to see. Hubbard, however, is a regular site on cruises to Alaska. Its nickname is the "galloping glacier," since it moves almost fast enough to see. Lucky ship passengers might see a massive chunk of the glacier fall off into Disenchantment Bay.

6. AMUNDSEN GLACIER ANTARCTICA, 80 MILES LONG

This glacier is named for the Norwegian explorer Roald Amundsen, who was the first man to reach the South Pole. In 1911, he led an expedition of men that walked for nearly four months across the frozen wasteland. Finally, on December 14, 1911, they took final measurements and realized they had done it. Others made the trip later, but Amundsen's group will always be the first.

5. NIMROD GLACIER ANTARCTICA, 84 MILES LONG

From the ground, glaciers look like huge sheets of ice. From space, however, their winding flows look like modern art. These images of the Nimrod Glacier could be in a museum.

4. BYRD GLACIER
ANTARCTICA, 85 MILES LONG

This is not the largest glacier, but it is one of the most studied. At more than 15 miles wide, and fast-moving enough to be measured, Byrd Glacier has revealed a lot to scientists. They have used radar to measure deep below the glacier to the ground beneath. These measurements help them see how glaciers are formed, how they move, and why they exist.

This glacier also brings with it a famous name. Admiral Richard Byrd was a famous polar explorer from the USA. He was the first person ever to fly an airplane over both the South and North Poles.

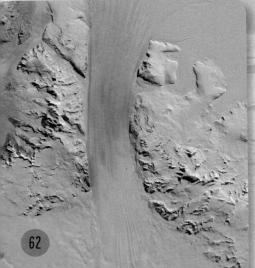

He earned his promotion to Admiral in the Navy after his South Pole flight in 1928. During that trip, he set up a camp called Little America that remains the base for a scientific outpost in use today. He made several further trips and spurred ongoing interest in polar research.

3. BERING GLACIER
ALASKA, 118 MILES LONG

This is the largest glacier in North America. Though not a usual cruise ship sight, it can be reached by kayak. Visitors can paddle near (but not too near!) the huge stack of ice as it touches into Vitus Lake.

2. BEARDMORE
ANTARCTICA, 125 MILES LONG

Dinosaurs at the South Pole? Well, maybe not all the way there, but close. Scientists have found fossils deep within Beardmore that show reptiles and animals that lived there long, long ago, when the South Pole was as warm as South America!

1. LAMBERT GLACIER
ANTARCTICA, 270 MILES LONG

To you and me, moving a mile in a year would be pretty slow. For a glacier, however, that's a world record. Lambert is not only the world's longest glacier, it's among the widest at 60 miles, and it's the fastest, too, with top speeds of almost a mile in a year. It might also be the deepest, too. At the center, radar has measured its depth at 8,200 feet, which is almost 2 miles!

LARGEST SPORTS STADIUMS

All around the world, people pack into huge stadiums to watch soccer, football, the Olympics, and other big sporting events. Sites where people watch horse or car races can actually fit even more people in, but for this list, we're talking enclosed stadiums. So grab your binoculars and your sunscreen, and we'll see you at the seats! The numbers listed are the official capacity (though most places can pack in a few more!).

10. TEXAS MEMORIAL STADIUM
AUSTIN, TEXAS, HOLDS 100,119

Home of the University of Texas Longhorns football team, the stadium is a sea of burnt orange on Saturdays during the fall—that's the team's uniform color, and everyone in the stands wears it, too!

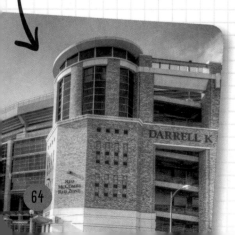

9. BRYANT–DENNY STADIUM
TUSCALOOSA, ALABAMA, HOLDS 101,821

The entire population of Tuscaloosa is just 95,000, so on a game day for the University of Alabama Crimson Tide, the stadium houses more people than the city!

8. Neyland Stadium
Knoxville, Tennessee, holds 102,037

Popular among students and fans for its great sight lines, Neyland is home to the University of Tennessee Volunteers. It also plays host to concerts and even a political rally or two!

7. Tiger Stadium
Baton Rouge, Louisiana, holds 102,321

It's hard for visiting teams to play in the din created by all the Louisiana State University Tigers football fans. The site's nickname is "Death Valley."

6. Ohio Stadium
Columbus, Ohio, holds 102,329

Say "The Horseshoe" to any college football fan, and they'll instantly know what you mean. Ohio State University plays its home football games in this U-shaped stadium.

5. AT&T Stadium
Arlington, Texas, holds 105,000

The newest stadium on this list, AT&T opened in 2009 to be the home of the NFL's Dallas Cowboys. It was believed to cost more than $1 billion to build and stretches nearly the length of the field. Along with Cowboys games, the stadium holds concerts, soccer games, WrestleMania, motorcycle races, and much more.

4. Estadio Azteca
Mexico City, holds 105,064

This massive building in the heart of Mexico's largest city hosted the FIFA World Cup finals of 1970 and 1986, the only place in the world with that honor.

3. Beaver Stadium
University Park, Pennsylvania, holds 107,282

Hordes of Penn State University fans turn Beaver Stadium white (with their clothing) when they pack into it for fall football afternoons.

2. Michigan Stadium
Ann Arbor, Michigan, holds 109,901

America's largest sports stadium fills with maize-and-gold-clad fans when the University of Michigan Wolverines play. Capacity is nearly 110,000, but with a little squeezing, a record of 115,109 was set in 2013. Known as the "Big House," Michigan Stadium was built in 1927, but has been renovated several times since.

Biggest Ever!

In 1954 for the World Cup Final, the Maracana Stadium in Rio de Janiero, Brazil was jam-packed with 199,854 people. That remains the most people ever to fill a single enclosed stadium for a sporting event. The enormous stadium was renovated in 2013. The new arrangement of seats reduced capacity dramatically—to just over 78,000. That's a bit more elbow room!

Indianapolis Motor Speedway

It's not a stadium, but it sure is huge! More than 300,000 people can pack into the enormous Indianapolis Motor Speedway. The stands go nearly all the way around the 2.5-mile long track. Since 1911, it's been the home of the famous Indy 500 auto race. Since 1994, the Brickyard 400 NASCAR race has also been held there. The track surface used to be made completely of bricks, but now just a single ceremonial strip remains at the finish line.

1. RUNGNADO MAY FIRST
PYONGYANG, NORTH KOREA, HOLDS 150,000

North Korea claims the title for the largest sports stadium, with this humongous sports palace. It opened in 1989, and its name refers to its site on the Rungra Island in the Taedong River. Soccer games are often played here, as well as track-and-field events that use the rubberized track that rings the grass field.

An enormous event called the Arirang Festival covers the field with dancers, acrobats, flags, floats, and more, sometimes involving more than 30,000 performers on the field. In 1995, the stadium claimed that a wrestling event drew 190,000 people, though it didn't say how they all managed to fit in there!

The stadium is designed to look like a magnolia flower, with wide, sweeping fabric panels set around the exterior. Since North Korea is basically a closed country, don't look for any World Cups or Olympic Games to be played there any time soon . . . but if they ever open up, they've got a huge stadium ready to use.

UNUSUAL BUILDINGS

Four walls and a roof weren't nearly exciting enough for the architects who created these wonders. They really thought out of the box when they designed these unusual buildings.

CRAZY HOUSE
DALAT, VIETNAM

The outside of this guesthouse looks like a large banyan tree, with mushrooms, spiderwebs, and caves carved into it. The rooms inside are themed for different animals, such as a tiger, an eagle, and a kangaroo.

THE IDEAL PALACE
HAUTERIVES, FRANCE

For years, mailman Ferdinand Cheval collected unusual rocks while he was making his rounds. After he retired, he spent the next 30 years using them to build his ideal—and highly unusual—palace.

GUGGENHEIM MUSEUM
BILBAO, SPAIN

Built of stone, glass, and titanium, this building is considered one of the world's most extraordinary examples of contemporary architecture.

Capital Gate
Abu Dhabi, United Arab Emirates

Feeling a little off-balance? Maybe that's because this 35-story skyscraper is designed to lean 18 degrees.

Lloyd's Building
London, England

Elevators, water pipes, and electric lines are all on the outside of this building. It is sometimes known as the "inside-out building"!

Sydney Opera House
Australia

This famous building with its shark-like fins on the top houses the performing arts center.

Music House
Huainan, China

It's easy to take note of this musical building. The escalators inside glass violins lead to the piano part of this house.

Guangzhou Circle
Ghuangzhou, China

Discs made from precious jade stone are valuable in Chinese culture, and the architects of this building designed it to mimic their shape.

Atomium
Brussels, Belgium

Imagine the chemical structure of an iron crystal. Can't? That's okay—the designers of the Atomium have done it for you, but this one is 165 billion times bigger.

SAGRADA FAMÍLIA
BARCELONA

The "Holy Family" Catholic church in Barcelona is big, at 295 feet tall and 197 feet wide. It is imposing, with 18 spires, and elaborate, with a unique mix of modern and Gothic architecture. However, it is still not finished. Construction started in 1882—that's 133 years ago—making this perhaps the world's longest-running construction project! But workers are now making progress. In 2010, they reached the halfway point. The goal is to be finished by 2026, the 100-year-anniversary of the death of Antoni Gaudí, the architect who designed it.

◄ **WHO'S IN CHARGE?**
Some of Gaudí's original blueprints for the church were destroyed by fire, so architects disagree about exactly what he had in mind. The current architect in charge says it doesn't matter too much because Gaudí never intended to have complete control over the design.

GUELL PARK

Barcelona's Guell Park was also designed by Gaudí. Built on a hill, the long walk to the top leads visitors past lush landscapes, fanciful buildings, and colorful sculptures.

MOST AMAZING THINGS BUILT BY HUMANS

Many of the lists in this book show you the wonderful work done by Mother Nature. Well, humans aren't too bad at building things either. Here's a look at some of the most astonishing building projects created by human beings. Some are new, some are very old, but all are AMAZING!

TAJ MAHAL

Built over 14 years and completed in 1648, this famous white-domed group of buildings is basically a tomb. Its builder wanted to honor his beloved wife, Mumtaz Mahal. He hired the best designers from around the Islamic world, and this is what they came up with. Try to memorize the full name of the builder: Al-Sultan al-'Azam wal Khaqan al-Mukarram, Abu'l-Muzaffar Shahab ud-din Muhammad, Sahib-i-Qiran-i-Sani, Shah Jahan I, Padshah Ghazi Zillu'llah.

GREAT WALL OF CHINA

It's not really one wall, but a series of connected walls built over a period of more than 2,000 years, ending in the 1400s. It stretches from east to west across a large part of China, with a total length of more than 13,170 miles.

EIFFEL TOWER

Designed and named for Gustave Eiffel, this famous landmark in Paris opened in 1889. For a while, it was the tallest man-made structure in the world until skyscrapers surpassed it. At night, it is lit with thousands of twinkling lights.

MACHU PICCHU

Nestled high atop a mountain in the Peruvian Andes, this amazing set of buildings was built by the Incas, and then abandoned. Not until Hiram Bingham was led there by native people in 1911 did the world once again see this marvel of early architecture.

MT. RUSHMORE

One man's obsession has become a nation's most famous sculpture. American sculptor Gutzon Borglum designed and supervised the building of a massive North Dakota mountainside into the heads of four United States presidents: George Washington, Abraham Lincoln, Theodore Roosevelt, and Thomas Jefferson.

STONEHENGE

Why was Stonehenge built about 5,000 years ago in England? No one knows for sure. Was it a temple? An astronomical clock? A site for rituals? The tall blocks of stone remain a popular tourist site millennia later.

STATUE OF LIBERTY

Few sculptures are more symbolic of a nation than this statue is of the United States. It was created by Gustave Eiffel, giving him two structures on this list. Opened in 1886, the statue in New York Harbor on Liberty Island glows at night with huge floodlights.

COLOSSEUM

Built in 80 CE, this ancient building is a reminder of ancient Rome in the middle of a busy modern-day city. When used by the ancients, it was the site of gladiator battles, animal fights, and other entertainments. Today, it is one of the world's most visited tourist sites.

FORBIDDEN CITY

The centerpiece of this sprawling Beijing site is 114 buildings that make up the Imperial Palace. There are more than 10,000 rooms in the entire set of buildings, which were home to China's emperors for 500 years. Why Forbidden? Common people were not allowed to mix with the emperors. Today, it is open to visitors.

THE GREAT PYRAMIDS

The Great Pyramids at Giza, Egypt, are the only one of the Seven Wonders of the Ancient World still standing. Deep inside the massive structures are the tombs of ancient Egyptian pharaohs. The largest of the three pyramids in the group was built by Khufu (also called Cheops) in about 2500 BCE. Slaves, guided by expert builders, were forced to move 2.3 million enormous blocks of stone for years to create the pyramids.

The site includes three major pyramids. The tallest is 481 feet tall and 755 feet wide at its base. Other pyramids in the complex were for Khufu's son, Khafre, and Khafre's son Menkaure.

MEET THE NEIGHBOR!

Located on the same plain of sand near the pyramids is another amazing ancient sculpture: the Sphinx. This seated figure, with the head of a man and the body of a lion, is from ancient Egyptian mythology. Though it has lost its nose, it retains its mystery, since no one is exactly sure why it was built here 3,500 years ago.

◄ READING THE WALLS

How do archaeologists know so much about who and how the temples were built? This is because the builders left a record. Using a style of writing called hieroglyphics, the builders decorated tomb walls with information about the pharaoh, his world, and the marvels he created. Scientists have been studying these ancient marvels since the Greeks and Romans arrived in the area.

10 LONGEST RIVERS ON THE PLANET

Believe it or not, there is some argument among scientists about this list. Deciding exactly where a river starts and ends is not as easy as you might think!

10. MEKONG
SOUTHEAST ASIA

The steamy Mekong flows from its origin in China through several Asian nations before emptying into the South China Sea. 2,749 miles.

9. RIO DE LA PLATA–PARANA
SOUTH AMERICA

In South America, the Amazon gets all the attention, but this river in Uruguay, Argentina, and Brazil is pretty impressive, too. It flows from south to north, as do most rivers in the Southern Hemisphere. 2,796 miles.

8. CONGO
AFRICA

Africa's second-longest river, the Congo, was once known as the Zaire River after the former name of its country of origin. It meanders for nearly 3,000 miles before emptying into the Atlantic Ocean. 2,900 miles.

7. HUANG HE CHINA

The ancient Chinese called this mighty waterway simply "The River." It helped support millions of people for centuries. It is also called the "Yellow River" thanks to the heavy sediment that colors the water for much of its length. 3,395 miles.

6. YENISEY–ANGARA–SELENGA Russia

Though one of the world's longest rivers, it is also one of the most remote. This three-river system flows through thousands of miles of pretty much nothing in central Russia before emptying into the Kara Sea. 3,448 miles.

5. OB–IRTYSH
Asia

For about half the year, it is easier to skate on this river than to sail on it. Its north Asian location—China, Kazakhstan, and Russia—means it freezes over during the harsh winter. 3,459 miles.

4. MISSISSIPPI–MISSOURI USA

The mighty Mississippi and the wandering Missouri cover most of the central and western United States before emptying at New Orleans into the Gulf of Mexico. The Lewis & Clark expedition traveled the Missouri in 1804 to "discover" the West. 3,709 miles.

3. YANGTZE
China and Tibet

Pouring through central China, the Yangtze touches as much area as four Californias put together. Along with some amazing animals, such as the rare river dolphin, the river is vital for producing power, carrying goods, and amazing tourists. 3,964 miles.

2. AMAZON South America

Thousands of smaller streams and creeks pour together out of the Amazon rainforest to create the world's second-longest river. The enormous basin drained by the Amazon is one of the most diverse places on the planet. Millions of species of plants and animals live only there, nourished by the mighty river. 4,049 miles.

1. NILE
AFRICA

The undisputed champion among world rivers, the Nile carves its way through 11 African countries before pouring into the Mediterranean Sea. For thousands of years, the Nile has supported the people living on its banks. Ancient Egyptians figured out its flood patterns in order to water their fields and grow the crops they needed to live. In 1970, the Aswan High Dam was built on the Nile to control the flooding more accurately as well as provide electrical power. The dam created the enormous Lake Nasser. Additional important branches of the Nile include the White Nile and the Blue Nile. 4,160 miles.

OTHER NAMES FOR THE NILE

Aur (ancient Egyptian)
Iaro (Coptic)
Kemi (alternate ancient Egyptian)
Aigyptos (Greek)
Nahr Al-Nil (Arabic)

FINDING THE SOURCE

Another name for the beginning of a river is the source. For hundreds of years, people wondered where the source of the Nile was. In 1858, British explorer John Hanning Speke correctly traced the river to Lake Victoria, from which it begins its journey north. Lake Victoria is the second-largest freshwater lake in the world.

SMALLEST COUNTRIES BY SIZE

Map lovers will need a magnifying glass to check out these tiny spots. From tiny islands to ancient fortress city-states, these are the smallest countries in the world as measured by land mass. There are some colonies and islands that would have made this list, but we included only fully independent nations.

10. MALDIVES
115 SQ. MILES

Located in the Indian Ocean, the Maldives is made up of a small group of islands. They are very low-lying islands, and its government fears that rising seas might someday swallow the country whole!

9. ST. KITTS AND NEVIS
104 SQ. MILES

This two-island nation in the Caribbean Sea might earn two spots on the list some day. Many on Nevis want to split and form their own island nation.

8. MARSHALL ISLANDS
70 SQ. MILES

Independent from the USA since 1986, it's best known as the home of one of the world's first and most active nuclear testing sites.

7. LIECHTENSTEIN
61 SQ. MILES

Famous for its banking services, this European landlocked country is officially a principality; that is, its head of state is a prince.

5. SINT MAARTEN
13 SQ. MILES

Long a colony of the Netherlands, in 2010 this Caribbean island became an independent country.

3. NAURU 8.5 SQ. MILES

Bird poop made this tiny spot in the South Pacific famous. People came from around the world to mine phosphate, an important mineral created in part by what birds leave behind!

2. MONACO 0.7 SQ. MILE

Glamorous and rich, Monaco is home to only 30,000 people. The entire country could fit into New York City's Central Park with room to spare. Founded on a fort built in 1215, the nation has been ruled by the Grimaldi family since 1419. A famous car race is held in its streets every year, and its harbor is filled with enormous yachts.

6. SAN MARINO
24 SQ. MILES

This tiny country surrounded by Italy claims to be founded way back in the year 301 CE and calls itself the "oldest republic in the world."

4. TUVALU
9 SQ. MILES

Small, but smart. In 2000, the nation rented its internet country code—.tv—for $50 million!

1. VATICAN CITY

0.2 SQ. MILES

Though it is surrounded not just by the city of Rome, but by Italy—and it's even called a "city"—the Vatican is in fact an independent country. Its leader is the Pope, who is also the leader of the Roman Catholic Church, which has its headquarters in Vatican City. The Vatican has less than 1,000 permanent residents, but it has its own coins and money, its own stamps, and its own bank. The Vatican's official name is the Holy See, and it has been home to Popes since the late 1300s. The Church used to control much more territory, but over the years it shrank to just the area around the Vatican buildings. Since 1929, Vatican City has officially been an independent country.

OTHER CITY-STATES

A city-state is a unit of government in which the entire "state" is made up of only one city. In ancient times, there were many city-states, such as Thebes in Egypt. Famous ancient Greek city-states included Athens, Sparta, and Corinth. Some scholars call the Mayan city of Chichen Itza a city-state. Today, Vatican City, Singapore, and Monaco are all considered city-states.

▶ MEET THE POPE

Pope Francis I lives in Vatican City in special apartments that look over St. Peter's Square. The enormous building on the square is St. Peter's Basilica. Pope Francis meets with visitors in Vatican City at events called "audiences." Often he will bless or address enormous crowds that fill the square. The home of the Pope is one of the most popular tourist destinations in Rome.

83

Weird Roadside Attractions

America is a big country, and people love to drive around to see it. Along the millions of miles of roads, some creative and enterprising people have put up "attractions" to draw driving visitors to their businesses. There are thousands to choose from. Here are some of the most famous or most interesting.

World's Largest Ball of Twine

We can't tell you how big this massive string ball is, since the owners in Cawker City, Kansas, are constantly adding to it. However, we can say that it includes more than 1.7 million feet of twine. It was started in 1953 and has surpassed many rivals for the crown.

World's Largest Baseball Bat

No one would be able to swing this mighty stick! The Hillerich and Bradsby company, makers of the famous Louisville Slugger wood baseball bat, built this monster in 1995. It stands at 120 feet tall alongside the company factory in Louisville, Kentucky.

Lucy the Elephant

This is one of the oldest roadside attractions on the list, first built in 1881. Lucy weighs 90 tons and stands at more than 60 feet tall. She's so big inside that she has been the site of a real estate office, a bar, and now a place for tourists to wander around in. Say "hi" to Lucy next time you're in Margate, New Jersey.

Corn Palace

Buildings can be made of brick, concrete, wood, mud, metal, and, of course, corn! This large building covered entirely with corn and corn-related products opened in 1895 in Mitchell, South Dakota. Its panels and murals are renewed each year to keep the corn fresh (and to bring tourists back year after year!).

The Basket Building

When your company's main product is baskets, you want everyone to know about it. So that's why the Longaberger Basket Company has its headquarters in Newark, Ohio, in a 192-foot long basket! Complete with handles, the huge building looks like something a giant might have left behind after lunch!

Wall of Gum

Tired of waiting in line for a movie, people in Seattle stuck their gum to a wall. That started in the late 1990s, and today the Post Alley Wall of Gum is one of Seattle's biggest—and grossest—attractions! Tens of thousands of germy, sticky, gooey pieces of gum are slapped on the wall. Yes, it really is as gross as it sounds!

Tallest Thermometer

In Baker, California, the temperature regularly tops 100°F. In 1990, the people of Baker built a thermometer that towers 134 feet over the tiny town in the Mojave Desert to display these scorching temperatures. The thermometer can be seen from miles away!

Cadillac Ranch

In the 1970s, a group of artists called the Ant Farm were looking for a way to create a piece of art that would stand the test of time. A rich guy named Stanley Marsh was ready to back them. The result is one of the most famous roadside attractions in the world—The Cadillac Ranch.

The artists bought (with Stanley's money) ten classic Cadillacs, all with the famous high tail fins of the 1950s and early 1960s. Then they buried the cars nose down. Soon, many people came to see this unusual piece of artwork, but they felt that they either had to add to it or take something away. Over the coming decades, dozens of pieces of the cars were taken away as souvenirs. People also began painting the cars with their own designs. Layer upon layer of spray paint graffiti turned the once plain cars into ever-changing murals.

Timber!

Built in 1991, in Nackawic, New Brunswick, this enormous axe salutes the Canadian lumber industry. Its handle is 50 feet long, while the huge (and sharp!) blade is 23 feet wide.

Off to Australia!

Roadside attractions are mostly a North American thing. However, Down Under in Australia, there's also a tradition of building big things and putting them on display for travelers to see. It started with the Big Scotsman in Adelaide. He stands at 16.4 feet tall outside Scotty's Motel. Since he was built in 1963, he has been joined by enormous statues of an amazing mix of things. Standing tall in places all over Australia are these large things: a lobster, a shrimp, a Merino sheep, a penguin, a cigar, a golf ball, a banana, a sapphire ring, and Captain Cook, not to mention a boxing crocodile, and dozens more.

Visitors come from around the world to marvel at this unusal creation, and to add their own coats of paint to the ranch. Why do they do this? Why not?

Cadillac Followers

Of course, when someone gets a good idea, others follow along soon after. Once the Cadillac Ranch became an American icon, other places wanted to attract visitors with their own car-related displays. Here are a few knockoffs:

Carhenge, Alliance, Nebraska: Yes, it's like the world-famous ancient monument Stonehenge, made out of cars.

Slug Bug Ranch, Panhandle, Texas: Don't like buried Cadillacs? How about buried Volkswagen Beetles?

SpiderBug, Lexington, Oklahoma:
A sculptor decided to put giant metal spider legs on the body of a Volkswagen Beetle.

WEIRDEST HOTELS

There are plenty of motels or chain hotels that you can stay at in which every room looks almost exactly the same. But next time you travel, why not step outside of your comfort zone a little and look into something like the very unusual hotels on this list. Convince your parents that staying inside a dog, or in the big toe of a Chinese god, or dining with giraffes is more fun!

10. Dog Bark Inn
USA

Your vacation will be a really unique one if you stay in this giant but cozy beagle. That's right, a room inside a giant dog, created by a couple in Idaho, USA, who are also professional chainsaw carvers. Their specialty—carved dog statues.

9. No Man's Fort
England

Just off the southern coast of England is a narrow body of water called the Solent. In the middle of it is a round fort first used in the 1880s. Today, it's a hotel and party island that can only be reached by boat.

8. Ice Hotel
Finland

Don't try to book this hotel in the summer! Every winter, artist Yngve Bergqvist carves a new ice hotel from blocks of glacial ice. When spring comes, the hotel melts and disappears! Actually, there are some rooms that are not made of ice and are also open during the summer.

7. Madonna Inn USA

No two rooms are the same at the wacky and whimsical Madonna Inn. Built into the side of a small hill alongside the busy 101 freeway in central California, the Madonna Inn is a wonderland of colors and creativity. Room themes include cave, golf, flowers, jungle, and 1950s, as well as rooms themed for places around the world, including Mexico, Switzerland, Ireland, Italy, Japan, and more.

6. Hotel Marqués de Riscal
Spain

World-famous architect Frank Gehry is known for museums and concert halls. But one of his buildings welcomes travelers. This hotel in Spain's wine country features the dramatic, swooping metal panels that Gehry loves. The area is beautiful, but the hotel's one-of-a-kind style is the main draw.

5. Tianzi Hotel
China

Are these three giant statues of Chinese gods . . . or a hotel? They're both! Visitors to this unique hotel in Hebei Province actually climb inside the enormous statues of Fu, Lu, and Shou. The front door is in Shou's left foot!

4. Amsterdam Zaandamn
The Netherlands

The Dutch city of Amsterdam is filled with colorful and cute buildings. The owners of this hotel decided to put many of those buildings together. Their hotel looks as though a giant gathered up a stack of houses and glued them together!

3. Featherbed Railroad USA

Some people take a train to get to their vacation spot. People who stay here can stay in a train. A hotel owner in Clear Lake, northern California, has turned nine antique railroad cars into rooms.

2. GIRAFFE MANOR KENYA

Have you ever had a giraffe steal your waffle? You might if you stay at this historic building on the plains near Nairobi. Giraffes live on the property and often stick their heads into second story windows seeking treats. Nearby game reserves mean you can see many other amazing animals.

CAPSULE HOTELS IN JAPAN

Have you ever slept in a cocoon? That's sort of what it feels like in the capsule hotels in Japan. Land and building space are very hard to find in Japan as it's a very crowded country. Traveling businessmen often just need a little place to sleep, and these unique hotels give them just that! Visitors climb into long, thin tubes not much bigger than a bed. No windows, just an opening at the end of the tube. Don't stay here if you're claustrophobic!

OTHER TREE HOTELS

Climbing up into a treehouse is a great part of being a kid. Some people who remember that fun have built treehouse hotels. Along with the one in the Amazon, here are a few others you can try:

TSALA TREETOP LODGE, SOUTH AFRICA
You can even have a nighttime marshmallow roast in your in-room fireplace.

OUT 'N' ABOUT TREEHOUSE TREESORT, OREGON
Yes, it's a "tree-sort," with more than a dozen separate treehouses. Many are connected by walkways or even zip lines!

TRANQUIL RESORT, INDIA
This place is not named very well. The rainforest where this treehouse hotel is built is home to howler monkeys, one of the loudest animals on Earth.

1. ARIAU AMAZON TOWERS BRAZIL

High above the treetops of the Amazon rainforest, you'll have a bird's-eye view of the trees at the Ariau Amazon Towers in Manaus, Brazil. The hotel was built on platforms and walkways high in the canopy of a forest next to the Amazon River. You can even swim in a pool built at the top of a tree!

Built in 1987, the resort now includes many buildings, connected by walkways. From the walkways, visitors can see exotic birds, mammals, and reptiles that live only in the rainforest.

In the jungles below, you can take walks or canoe rides (watch out for piranha!). Unlike the animals, though, you won't have to forage for your own food. The hotel has several restaurants where you can eat and look around from this unique viewpoint!

Most Amazing Ocean Occurrences

The waters of the world's oceans cover 70 percent of the surface of the Earth. So it's not surprising that in such an enormous space some pretty unusual and unique things occur. Here's a look at some of the bizarre and sometimes scary things that can happen or exist in the world's oceans.

10. The Milky Sea

In the Indian Ocean, a swirl of glowing bacteria (see bioluminescence, below) can turn patches of the water a milky white color.

9. Meeting of the Seas

Off a peninsula in Denmark, two large seas, the Skagerrak and the Kattegat, meet. When two bodies of water meet, they mix easily. But these two seas are so different—one is very salty, the other is not—they form a clear line of two different colors.

8. Salty Death

Brine is super-salty water. In the Arctic, when seawater freezes, the salt from the water drifts to the bottom. As it does so, it can form long tubes of freezing brine. As they reach the bottom, they instantly freeze and kill any animals caught in their icy grip.

7. Bioluminescence

The ocean can sometimes glow with light, called bioluminescence, which is created by tiny animals that give off their own light. When they gather near the surface at night, the sea takes on an eerie glow!

6. Red Tide

Algae are plants that live in the ocean. Sometimes, they grow suddenly in huge quantities. They can become so thick near coastlines that they can harm fish, birds, and even people who enter the water. Often, the blooms of algae are colored, so they have all taken on the name "red tide."

5. Undersea Volcanoes

Deep beneath the sea is land. In many places, there are mountains and ridges at the bottom. There are also volcanoes. They send magma and lava out, forming a new sea bottom. The super-heated water near these volcanoes also gives life to some strange marine creatures, some of which can survive without light, such as the black dragonfish.

4. Gyres

While a whirlpool is more local, a gyre is enormous. As the Earth spins, the force of the spinning moves the waters of the oceans. Add in the currents that are moving due to wind and land, and the result is an enormous circular gyre. One of the largest encircles almost the entire Pacific Ocean.

3. Whirlpools

When two powerful ocean currents meet, their opposing power can create a huge, spinning whirlpool. Most are not dangerous, but some are still rather strong.

2. Plastic Islands

Thanks to the billions of tons of trash we put in the ocean each year, enormous floating islands of plastic garbage float around in the Pacific Ocean. Some can be miles wide, endangering marine life and shipping. Let's start recycling!

1. WATERSPOUTS

On land, tornadoes can cause great damage. When they happen over water, they create an amazing spectacle, and you still would not want to get in their way. Waterspouts are caused, like tornadoes, by fast-spinning winds. As the winds spin over ocean or lake water, they can actually suck the water up toward the clouds. The result looks like a thin, white tube snaking up into the sky.

There are actually two kinds of waterspouts. One type forms during storms, much like a tornado. The Florida Keys, USA, is a great place to spot these. The winds start from the clouds and pull the water up to make a spout that can be hundreds of feet high.

Another type of waterspout happens during calmer weather. In lighter winds, the spout can appear to rise up from the water's surface, stretching up to meet the clouds above. These are usually not as strong or as long-lasting, so keep your camera ready!

THE ROARING FORTIES AND THE FAST FIFTIES

Numbered latitude lines show where you are located on the surface of the Earth. The number gets higher as you go south or north of the Equator. From 40–50 degrees of south latitude, the winds that whirl around the Earth create some of the biggest waves and sea storms in the world. Yet that's where ships can also move around the world fastest. Sailors looking for faster winds and bigger seas go fifty degrees south, where only the largest ships can survive the powerful winds.

WORLD'S BIGGEST TIDE!

Tides happen when the moon's gravity pulls bodies of water back and forth from a shoreline. They happen on very precise schedules, with two high tides and two low tides every 24 hours. Most tides do not have a huge effect on the shoreline. However, in the Bay of Fundy in Nova Scotia, Canada, the tide is enormous. At the right time of year, you can see the water at low tide drop more than 50 feet from the high tide mark.

UNUSUAL MODES OF TRANSPORTATION

Cars? Boring! Walking? Been there, done that. Bicycles? Everybody's got one. What if you're looking for a more unusual and interesting way to get around? We've got the list for you. These are some of the coolest, most unique ways to move around from place to place.

MAG-LEV TRAINS

These super-fast trains are not that unusual, but the way they move is amazing. Instead of an engine turning wheels on a track, these trains are pulled along by the power of magnets. The current flowing through a track attracts the magnets below each car and takes the trains to the fastest speeds in the world.

OSTRICH

The world's largest birds are probably not a good idea for a long ride, but are great for a fun and feathery spin around the track. A ranch in South Africa offers ostrich rides, and also trains the birds for professional racing events.

SEGWAY

Riding a Segway is an easy and convenient way to get around. Popular for tours of cities, Segways were invented in 2001 by Dean Kamen. Run by electricity, they are zippy, quick, and easy to ride.

Giant Unicycle

The tallest unicycle ever ridden was 115 feet from seat to ground, but Sem Abrahams only rode it a few feet in 2004. For regular riders, the largest has a 36-inch wheel beneath a comfy seat for one-wheeling around town.

Hyperbike

Invented by Curtis DeForest, this weird machine is referred to as the HyperBike. It has 8-foot wheels that are at an angle, not straight up and down. The rider uses both arms and legs to pedal, and there is no seat. The rider hangs in a harness. DeForest claims it can go up to 50 miles per hour!

Hovercraft

Riding across water on a cushion of air, hovercraft were seen at one point as the solution for sea travel. The rides were not as smooth as first thought, though, and today only one hovercraft makes regular ferry runs in England.

Duck Boats

What do you call a machine that's a truck . . . and a boat? A duck boat! Made famous in Boston as part of the Red Sox parades, duck boats are now found in many seaside cities. Tourists see the town by land, and then roll into the water for a watery tour, too.

Madeira Toboggans

If a tourist goes up to the top of the city of Funchal on the Mediterranean island of Madeira, he or she can come down in a very interesting way. Since the 1850s, wicker toboggans have sped down the steep streets leading to the waterfront. Today, tourists are the only ones who use them, guided by a pair of white-clad experts. The 1.2-mile trip takes about 10 minutes.

CAMBODIA BAMBOO TRAIN

In Cambodia, creative local folks have built flat bamboo platforms atop old rail cars to create a fast and easy way to get around. On a single track, the trains, called "norries," are run by small motors and carry passengers and freight back and forth.

THE ICE ANGEL

If you live on an island on a lake that freezes, what do you do in winter? On Madeline Island in Wisconsin, you can call on the Ice Angel. This special ice boat skims across or through the ice when the water ferry can no longer operate.

THE IDITAROD

The most famous dog-sled race in the world is the Iditarod. It was first held in 1973 to honor the men and dogs who saved the children of Nome back in 1925 (see the story of Balto on the next page). That event was a relay, but the Iditarod is a multi-day race with the same team of dogs and only one musher (driver). The route changes each year, but is at least 1,000 miles long and takes more than ten days. Rick Swenson has won the race five times, the most of any musher.

DOG SLEDS

When the ice and snow are too much for people to walk through, dogs are the answer. For thousands of years, people in the far north have been using dogs pulling sleds to get around. Dogs are hitched like horses to the front of wooden sleds. As their strong, furry paws dig into the ice and snow, the dogs pull the sleds and the driver (known as a musher). Huskies are the most common sled dogs, but other breeds can be trained, as long as they have the thick fur coats needed to withstand the icy cold. Sled dogs used to be the normal way of getting around, but with the invention of snowmobiles, they are now more for racing and tourism than daily use.

THE STORY OF BALTO

In 1925, a terrible outbreak of diptheria (a nasty disease) hit the tiny town of Nome, Alaska. Medicine was needed right away. However, because it was winter, planes could not land and ships could not break through the ice. So, teams of sled dogs created a relay to bring the medicine in time. Dozens of dogs took turns over more than 1,000 miles of frozen ground, snowy forest, and icy lakes. The most famous sled-puller was a Siberian husky named Balto, whose courage became the symbol of the event. A statue of Balto stands in New York's Central Park in his memory.

MOST INTERESTING ISLANDS

Islands conjure up images of sandy beaches, blue water, and waving palm trees. Sure, there are a lot of those tropical paradises in the world, but not all islands are like that. You might not be able to work on a tan on some of these islands, but you can get an interesting story.

10. PITCAIRN ISLAND
SOUTHERN PACIFIC OCEAN

The 48 residents of Pitcairn Island are descended from sailors who staged a mutiny on an English ship called the HMS *Bounty* in 1789.

9. PALMYRA ATOLL
USA

The Palymra Atoll (a group of islands) is a magnet for mystery and mayhem. Over the years there have been murders, shipwrecks, unexplained ghostly lights, and more. Other than that, it's an island paradise. . . .

8. ISLAND OF THE DOLLS MEXICO

When a little girl drowned here decades ago, the island's only resident put a doll in a tree to make her soul happy. Since then, more people have hung dolls in trees all over the island.

7. PALM JUMEIRAH
DUBAI, UAE

One of three man-made islands off the coast of Dubai, this island is the largest artificial island in the world and is built in the shape of a palm tree.

6. North Sentinel Island Bay of Bengal

Don't plan a visit here. The native people who live here do not want contact with other civilizations. They shoot arrows and throw rocks at people who try to come ashore.

4. Hashima Japan

The coal mining industry once let 5,000 people live on Hashima Island in Japan. Now it's abandoned, but the buildings left behind give a glimpse into life several decades ago.

3. Socotra Island Yemen

The umbrella-shaped dragon's blood tree (named for its red sap) gives this island an other-worldly appearance. The island has about 700 plant and animal species that can be found nowhere else on earth.

5. Bishop Rock Isles of Scilly

The *Guinness Book of World Records* lists Bishop Rock as the smallest island with a building— a lighthouse. The island is only 151 feet long and 52.5 feet wide. So, football's out.

2. Alcatraz Island USA

From 1934 to 1963, the US government used this island near San Francisco, California, to run a high-security prison for bank robbers, murderers, and other dangerous criminals. Escape attempts were common—and mostly unsuccessful.

1. EASTER ISLAND
CHILE

The Rapa Nui people from Polynesia first came to Easter Island about 1,000 years ago and built a thriving society. They built something even more amazing, too—huge statues called *moai*. There are 887 of these statues carved to look like giant human heads. Made from the volcanic rocks on the island, these statues are about 13 feet tall and about 5 feet across at the base. And they're *really* heavy—about 13.8 tons. Archaeologists still aren't sure how these ancient peoples had the tools and technology to build and move such massive statues.

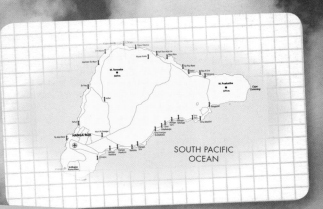

▶ A LONG TRIP
Easter Island is a long way from anywhere. The nearest island is faraway Pitcairn, which is 1,289 miles away—and it only has 50 people living on it.

SOUTH PACIFIC OCEAN

PERUVIAN SLAVE TRADE

In 1862, slave traders from Peru came to Easter Island to take the inhabitants and turn them into slaves. They took 1,500 people, about half of the island's population. Most of them died, but a few managed to return to the island in 1863. Unfortunately, they brought smallpox with them—and that killed most of the remaining population. By 1877, only 111 people remained. That number has since gone back up. The island currently has a population of about 6,000 people.

Biggest Countries
That Are Islands

About ten percent of the world's population lives on an island. Some big countries are made up of groups of islands, such as Japan and the Philippines, but others are contained primarily on one main island. Some are big, some are small, but they are all independent!

Republic of Kiribati

The groups of islands that make up Kiribati (it's pronounced keer-uh-BAHS) are scattered across an area the size of the USA in the central Pacific Ocean.

Bahrain

Pearl fishing was the main industry of Bahrain for centuries—until oil was found in the 1930s.

Nauru

The world's smallest island country, Nauru, is only 8.1 square miles and completely surrounded by a coral reef. Located in the central Pacific.

Singapore

Things are very neat and orderly in Singapore, one of the world's top commercial centers. Maybe that's because it's illegal to chew gum!

Cuba

Located just 90 miles off the coast of Florida, Cuba is famous for producing sugar, cigars, and baseball players.

MADAGASCAR

Ring-tailed lemurs are one of the best-known species on this island. Thousands of plant and animal species are found on Madagascar. Most of them can be found nowhere else in the world.

ICELAND

Iceland is one of the most volcanically active places in the world. In 2010, a series of eruptions made so much ash that planes all across Europe had to stay on the ground until the dust settled.

JAMAICA

It doesn't snow on this tropical island nation, so it came as a surprise when the country put together a bobsled team that competed at the Winter Olympic Games.

SRI LANKA

The government of Sri Lanka is the oldest democracy on the Asian continent, formed in 1931.

AUSTRALIA

Native people called aboriginals have lived in Australia for close to 50,000 years, but European settlement only began in the late 1700s. That marks the strange beginning of Australia's modern history. In 1788, England wanted to get rid of its prisoners and decided to banish them to Australia. The idea was that Australia was too remote for the convicts to cause any more trouble to law-abiding citizens. Most of these convicts were not dangerous; they were guilty of small crimes, such as petty theft, or having the "wrong" political beliefs. It's estimated that some 20 percent of Australia's current population is descended from these "criminals."

▶ HOME SWEET HOME

By far the largest island in the world, Australia is often referred to as the land "Down Under" because of its location in the Southern Hemisphere. Few people live in the hot, desert interior though. Most of them are clustered in cities along the coasts. Sydney and Melbourne are Australia's two largest cities, and they are always competing with one another. The government didn't want to play favorites, so it made Canberra the capital city in 1908.

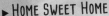

THE GREAT BARRIER REEF

One of Australia's crown jewels isn't even on the mainland. The world's largest coral reef, the Great Barrier Reef, stretches for 1,400 miles along Australia's northeast coast. It's so big it can even be seen from outer space! Billions of tiny animals called coral polyps actually created the reef with their bodies, making it the world's largest structure made up of living things.

LARGEST LAKES

When you stand on the shores of these lakes, you can't see the other side. It's like being next to an ocean . . . but without the saltwater! Lakes are formed by water flowing from streams and rivers into large basins. These are the largest lakes in the world, measured by surface area of the water in the lakes.

10. GREAT SLAVE LAKE
CANADA, 11,170 SQUARE MILES

You can drive across this far-northern lake in a huge truck, as it is nearly covered with thick ice for much of the winter. It's also North America's deepest lake at more than 2,000 feet.

9. NYASA
AFRICA, 11,600 SQUARE MILES

Surrounded by Malawi, Mozambique, and Tanzania in southeastern Africa, this also known as Lake Malawi. That nation claims most of the lake, but its neighbo dispute it. Steep mountains rise high above most of the edges of the lake.

8. GREAT BEAR LAKE
CANADA, 12,000 SQUARE MILES

If you stretched out the shoreline of Great Bear Lake, it would reach from Las Vegas to Chicago in the USA or from Vancouver to Regina in Canada. This is the largest lake that is located entirely within Canada.

7. LAKE BAIKAL
RUSSIA, 12,162 SQUARE MILES

If you drop something in Lake Baikal, you can kiss it goodbye! This is the deepest lake on the planet, with some sections of it dropping to almost a mile deep.

6. TANGANYIKA
AFRICA, 12,700 SQUARE MILES

On the border between Tanzania and the Democratic Republic of the Congo, this lake is the longest in the world (418 miles) as well as one of the oldest. Many of the species of fish that live in the lake can't be found anywhere else on Earth.

5. MICHIGAN
UNITED STATES, 22,400 SQUARE MILES

This is one of three of the Great Lakes in the top five worldwide. Michigan is the only one of the Great Lakes completely inside the United States. Its western border is Wisconsin, while its eastern is Michigan.

4. HURON
UNITED STATES AND CANADA, 23,010 SQUARE MILES

No. 4 on this list, but home to the largest freshwater island in the world, Manitoulin Island. The massive Georgian Bay section of Lake Huron would be on the top 20 of world lakes all by itself!

OFF THE LIST

Until 2014, the Aral Sea, a lake in central Asia, was the fourth-largest in the world, covering more than 13,000 square miles. Today, it's only about 10 percent of that size, depending on rainfall. Dams upstream on the rivers that fed the lake have cut off most of the water, and now it's a massive mud pit.

3. VICTORIA AFRICA, 26,828 SQUARE MILES

Hard to believe that Western explorers had trouble finding this enormous lake, but they did. Europeans looked for two centuries for the source of the River Nile before arriving at Lake Victoria in 1858. It was named for the English queen at that time.

2. SUPERIOR
UNITED STATES AND CANADA, 31,820 SQUARE MILES

How deep is Superior? The water from all of the other four Great Lakes—plus three more Lake Eries!—could fit inside Superior's enormous basin. It's a busy and sometimes dangerous shipping site, with huge boats carrying cargo across it. Shipwrecks have become popular underwater homes . . . for fish here!

MAKING LAKES

Where do the holes in the ground that become lakes come from? Many are pits dug by long-ago glaciers as they crawled across the land. Others were created when the massive plates covering the Earth shifted. Smaller lakes have been created by landslides that block a river. Other lakes are formed by humans when we build a dam on a river. Lake Mead in Nevada is one of those.

TYPE OF LAKES
If water flows into and out of a lake, then that lake is considered "open." The level of the lake might rise or fall, depending on how much water flows in. A closed lake does not have water flowing into or out of it. The Great Salt Lake in Utah is a closed lake. It became super-salty over the years because the only "new" water that enters it comes from rain. Over time, the solids in the water settled without new freshwater flowing through. The result is super-salty water.

1. CASPIAN SEA
152,238 SQUARE MILES

If it's called a sea, then why is it on this list of largest lakes? From a scientist's point of view, it's actually a lake because it is fed by rivers and streams and not connected to a larger body of water. To a politician in Russia or Iran, two of the countries that border the water, calling it a "lake" is also important. If it was a "sea," then international law could be enforced. If it's a lake, then the countries it touches divide it up among themselves. And since there is natural gas and oil found drilled beneath its waters, that decision is pretty important indeed! In fact, a 2014 treaty said just that and prevented foreign ships from operating on the Caspian, especially foreign military ships. So although it's been called "Sea" for thousands of years, it's a lake to its neighbors.

Apart from its value to those neighboring nations, some of the facts about this body of water are amazing:

- ONE THIRD OF THE WORLD'S LAKE WATERS ARE HELD HERE
- THE SURFACE AREA IS LARGER THAN THE ISLANDS OF JAPAN
- THE WATER IS MOSTLY SALTWATER OR BRACKISH WATER, NOT FULLY FRESHWATER
- IT IS A "CLOSED" LAKE (SEE LEFT)
- THE CASPIAN IS HOME TO FAMOUS STURGEON FISH, WHOSE EGGS ARE EATEN AS AN EXPENSIVE DISH CALLED CAVIAR
- THE CASPIAN SEAL LIVES ONLY IN THE BRACKISH WATERS OF THIS LAKE

Most Famous Festivals

Need a reason to celebrate? There are festivals for all kinds of things, from important holidays to old traditions. Some festivals are traditionally held in one place, and others are widespread, with celebrations in different places all over the world.

10. La Tomatina SPAIN

This one will have you seeing red! A food fight at a parade in 1945 has now evolved into an annual tradition in which people throw tomatoes at each other.

8. Harbin Ice and Snow Sculpture Festival CHINA

Elaborate ice and snow sculptures turn this Chinese city into a winter wonderland for several weeks each year.

7. Edinburgh Festival Fringe SCOTLAND

Musicians, dancers, comedians, and more put on more than 3,000 shows in less than a month at the largest performing arts festival in the world.

9. Albuquerque International Balloon Fiesta USA

Hot air balloon pilots compete in precision flying events during this fiesta, but most people just want to watch the spectacular sight of hundreds of colorful balloons in the morning skies.

6. Lantern Festival China

Children solve riddles written on lanterns during this festival, which comes at the end of the Chinese New Year celebration.

4. Holi India

The Hindu "festival of colors" celebrates the arrival of spring. It is held around the world wherever Hindus live, and the event features the tossing of heaps of colored powder. You can spot people celebrating as they might look like walking rainbows!

2. Oktoberfest Germany

It's two solid weeks of celebrating German food and culture during Oktoberfest. However, the largest festival, which is held in Munich, Germany, actually happens usually in September!

5. Day of the Dead Mexico

Dead but not forgotten—that's the idea behind this Mexican festival, when people remember their deceased loved ones.

3. San Fermin Festival Spain

Honoring one of Spain's patron saints, this festival's best-known event is the running of the bulls, when people try to outrun charging bulls on a narrow street in Pamplona.

1. CARNIVAL
BRAZIL

In the Christian religion, Jesus suffered for 40 days in the desert. Today this time period is recognized as Lent. Modern Catholics often deny themselves some physical pleasure during this time to remember Jesus's suffering. But before that—it's party time! Carnival celebrations happen all over the world, but they are perhaps most popular in Brazil. For almost a week in February, work life grinds to a halt in much of Brazil. Instead, people put on elaborate costumes, march in parades, sing, dance, and eat and drink to their heart's content.

MARDI GRAS

In the USA, the most famous Carnival celebration is Mardi Gras—and the city that does it best is New Orleans, Louisiana. Mardi Gras is French for "Fat Tuesday," because people eat a lot on the Tuesday before Ash Wednesday, the first day of Lent. The city of New Orleans had its first Mardi Gras in 1837, and in 1875 the state declared it a legal holiday. No school!

▶ GET MOVING

Carnivals would not be complete without the samba, a type of African–Brazilian dance. Special samba schools are located in various neighborhoods of large cities such as Rio de Janeiro. The people at the schools come up with ideas for parade floats and practice dances that they can perform when Carnival arrives.

Famous Castles

Old castles might get a bit drafty. The doors are heavy, and the dungeons are dark and gloomy. But if you've got a country to defend from conquering armies, you'll need one of these!

Segovia Castle
Spain

This castle has been a fortress, a royal palace, a prison, a military academy, and a museum. An unusual feature is its shape—it looks like the bow of a ship.

Himeji Castle
Japan

Dating back to 1333, Himeji Castle has 83 buildings and is an example of Japanese-style architecture from the country's feudal period.

Citadel of Aleppo
Syria

Most of this castle's construction dates from about the twelfth century, but the site itself has been used since the third millenium BCE.

Edinburgh Castle
Scotland

With its strategic position on a hill in the city, Edinburgh Castle played an important part in many wars in Scottish history.

Kronborg Castle
Denmark

This Renaissance-style castle dates back to the 1500s. William Shakespeare used it as the model for the castle in his famous play *Hamlet*.

MALBORK CASTLE
POLAND

This red brick castle is the largest in the world by surface area, measuring 1,545,600 square feet. A great place to play hide-and-seek!

BRAN CASTLE
TRANSYLVANIA, ROMANIA

With its striking red roofs, this castle resembles the one that the vampire Count Dracula lived in.

WINDSOR CASTLE
ENGLAND

Members of the British royal family have lived here for almost 1,000 years, making this the oldest continuously inhabited castle in Europe.

NEUSCHWANSTEIN CASTLE
BAVARIA, GERMANY

Look familiar? This is the castle that inspired Walt Disney's Sleeping Beauty castle. Built in the 1800s, this castle is relatively young by castle standards.

PRAGUE CASTLE
CZECH REPUBLIC

Originally built around the year 870 CE, Prague Castle is now the world's largest ancient castle. Actually, it's not just one building, but a whole complex of buildings that covers 753,000 square feet. That's about the size of seven football fields! Within its walls there are churches, residential areas, administrative buildings, museums, and even tombs. Several gardens surround the buildings. The architecture within the castle complex spans 1,000 years, ranging from early Roman-style buildings from the tenth century to Gothic styles from the medieval period in the 1300s.

SEVEN AND SEVEN

The priceless crown jewels of the Czech Republic are stored deep within Prague Castle, in an iron safe within a chamber in St. Vitus Cathedral. Both the safe and the room each have seven different locks, and the keys to the locks are given to seven different people. They all have to get together at the same time to access the jewels.

TENNIS, ANYONE?

Standing in the castle's Royal Garden is the Ball Game Hall, a huge, indoor sports arena built in 1569. Nobles used it to play an early form of tennis. Later it was turned into a stable, and today it is used for concerts and exhibitions.

Most Famous Museums

It's said that the ancient Greeks came up with the idea of museums. They built temples to honor their gods, and then filled them with art and sculptures. Many of today's famous museums were started by individuals or groups of people with small collections of art or antiques, but have grown over the years.

10. Metropolitan Museum of Art
New York, USA

Nicknamed "The Met," the largest art museum in the USA is known not only for art, but for its collections of arms and armor, costumes, and musical instruments.

9. National Palace Museum
Taipei, Taiwan

The ancient emperors of China had the money to buy the best things available, and now many of those artifacts are on display at Taiwan's National Palace Museum.

8. Vatican Museums
Vatican City, Rome, Italy

Some of the best examples of old Roman and medieval European art are on display at the 54 galleries of the Vatican Museums, including Michelangelo's masterpiece, the Sistine Chapel.

7. National Museum of Anthropology
Mexico City, Mexico

Walking around this museum feels like being in an *Indiana Jones* video game, with rare treasures from Mexico's ancient Mayan and Aztec civilizations.

6. National Museum of China
Beijing, China

China has one of the oldest civilizations on Earth, and this museum covers all of it—going back almost two million years.

5. Museo del Prado Madrid, Spain

Spain's national art museum displays European art from the twelfth to the nineteenth centuries, with an emphasis on Spanish art.

4. The British Museum London

No part of human culture is overlooked in the vast collections of the British Museum, which has eight million items and is one of the largest in the world.

3. Hermitage Museum
St. Petersburg, Russia

Catherine the Great, the empress of Russia, started this museum in 1764. It has the biggest collection of paintings anywhere in the world.

2. Smithsonian Institution
Washington, D.C., USA

The Natural History Museum and the Air and Space Museum are two of the most famous of the Smithsonian's museums, which includes 19 different museums altogether.

1. THE LOUVRE
PARIS, FRANCE

About ten million people visit the Louvre every year—some 26,000 every day—making it the world's most-visited museum. The Louvre was built in the 1100s and was originally used as a fortress. Later it became a home for French royalty. During the French Revolution of the 1790s, the French government decided that the Louvre building should be turned into a museum. It started with only 537 paintings, but now has more than 380,000 objects, dating from prehistory on up until the present time. It is especially known for its collections of Egyptian, Greek, and Roman artifacts.

ONE'S NOT ENOUGH

Some places want their own Louvre. A second Louvre museum opened in the city of Lens, France, in the mid-2000s, to help reduce the number of people crammed into the main one. Another Louvre is planned for Abu Dhabi in the United Arab Emirates.

A Famous Smile

Probably the world's most famous painting—the *Mona Lisa*—is displayed at the Louvre. Italian artist Leonardo Da Vinci painted this masterpiece in the early 1500s. Art scholars and regular people alike are captivated by the enigmatic smile on the face of the woman in the painting. Wonder what she was thinking?

DEADLIEST TORNADOES

Tornadoes are twisting, high-powered, fast-moving clouds that reach down from a storm to touch the ground. When that power hits buildings, trees, cars, or anything on the ground, the tornado wins every time. Today, weather experts can usually give an area good warning before a tornado hits. This has helped to reduce the number of deaths from tornadoes. New ways of building shelters and large structures have also created more safe havens for people and animals. But Mother Nature is still very powerful, so when tornadoes strike, taking shelter immediately is the only way to survive.

10. FLINT, MICHIGAN
JUNE 8, 1953–116 DEATHS

This tornado touched down just outside Tornado Alley (a wide, storm-heavy region of the American Great Plains). It also hit in the evening when many people were in bed. This combination made it the last single American tornado to claim 100 lives.

9. NEW RICHMOND, WISCONSIN
JUNE 12, 1899–117 DEATHS

A visiting circus had drawn a large crowd to this small Wisconsin town. When the tornado hit at about 6 p.m., the streets were full of people, who quickly panicked while looking for shelter. Much of the town was destroyed.

8. AMITE, LOUISIANA, AND PURVIS, MISSISSIPPI APRIL 24, 1908–143 DEATHS

This was actually two tornadoes, but the worst one did its damage over a long swath. The main twister traveled more than 150 miles, one of the longest distances recorded by a tornado.

7. JOPLIN, MISSOURI
MAY 22, 2011–158 DEATHS

The power of tornadoes is measured on the EF scale. A rating of 5 is the highest on the scale, and this twister earned that grade. Its winds topped 200 miles per hour as it roared through the crowded suburb.

6. WOODWARD, OKLAHOMA
APRIL 9, 1947–181 DEATHS

A massive, 1.8-mile wide tornado was one of several to hit the northeast of Oklahoma, in the heart of Tornado Alley. When it had passed through, a massive stone government building was the only structure left standing for blocks around.

5. GAINESVILLE, GEORGIA
APRIL 6, 1936–203 DEATHS

This small town got hit by the second of what was actually a pair of tornadoes. One witness said the midday sky "became as dark as night." More than 200 people were reported dead. However, at this time in the deep South, nobody counted how many African-Americans might have been killed, so this death toll was certainly much higher.

4. TUPELO, MISSISSIPPI
APRIL 5, 1936–216 DEATHS

The first of the deadly double hit Tupelo early on a Thursday. Over the next four days, other tornadoes wreaked havoc in the area, including Gainesville, Georgia. Its winds of more than 260 miles per hour might be the strongest ever.

125

3. St. Louis, Missouri
May 27, 1896—255 deaths

It's rare that a major tornado hits a large city. Mostly that's because cities don't take up as much room as the wide-open plains. However, when they do hit cities, they can do terrible damage, as this one did to St. Louis. The winds tore down part of a bridge and ripped through crowded streets, destroying hundreds of buildings.

2. Natchez, Mississippi
May 7, 1840—317 deaths

Natchez Landing was crowded on this day, but not with buildings—with boats. The Mississippi River port was packed with flatboats, steamboats, and all manner of watercraft. When the storm roared in, boats were crushed, and their crews drowned in the river. On land, the twister tore up the town's two churches. As with other Southern storms of this time period, the death toll did not include the black population of the area, so this number should be much higher.

Tornado Alley

Thanks to the wide open spaces of the Great Plains and the wind patterns that form large storms there, an area from Arkansas in the northwest to the Dakotas is known as Tornado Alley. Each year, hundreds of twisters touch down in this huge area of land. Residents there are always listening for the sirens that go off to warn of an approaching storm that might become a twister. The summer months are the worst, when rising heat from the ground adds to the winds to create perfect twister conditions.

EF Scale

Scientists measure tornadoes by wind speed on the Enhanced Fujita (EF) Scale. Here are the ranges of the sections of the scale:

EF No.	3-Second Gust of Wind
0	65-85 MPH
1	86-110 MPH
2	111-135 MPH
3	136-165 MPH
4	166-200 MPH
5	OVER 200 MPH

1. TRI-STATE TORNADO
MARCH 18, 1925—695 DEATHS

When a single tornado ravages parts of three states, it's one for the record books. This record-setting 1925 twister started in Missouri, raced across Illinois, and finally blew apart in Indiana—traveling a stunning distance of 219 miles. It reached almost unheard of speeds of more than 70 miles per hour. Along with the record for most deaths, it caused more than 13,000 injuries, thought to be a record as well. At least one town in each state was completely destroyed. Most of the dead were in southern Illinois, where the storm was strongest and stayed the longest. Murphysboro, Illinois, alone lost more than 230 people, about half of the town's residents.

Schools were destroyed, and churches lost their steeples. In Illinois, miners came out from work to find that the twister had smashed their houses while they worked unaware underground. A witness told the *St. Louis Post-Dispatch*, "The air was full of everything, boards, branches of trees, garments, pans, stoves, all churning around together. I saw whole sides of houses rolling along near the ground."

Modern tornado detection means that such deadly results might be avoided in the future.

INCREDIBLE NATIONAL CAPITAL BUILDINGS

Lots of people go to the office every day, but only a few get to go to work in amazing buildings like these. A country's government is one of the things that defines it, and these nations are proud to show off where decisions get made.

PARLIAMENT HOUSE
CANBERRA, AUSTRALIA

Architects designed this building in the shape of a boomerang, which was used as a hunting weapon by indigenous Australians.

HUNGARIAN PARLIAMENT
BUDAPEST, HUNGARY

Better late than never. The Hungarian Parliament Building opened for business in 1896—1,000 years after the formation of the country itself.

GREAT HALL OF THE PEOPLE
BEIJING, CHINA

Each province of China has its own section in the Great Hall, which was built by volunteers in less than a year.

THE REICHSTAG BUILDING
BERLIN, GERMANY

Germany used to be divided into two countries: East Germany was communist and West Germany was democratic. In 1990 they reunited with a democratic government. In 1999 the parliament began to meet in this building, which had not been used since the Second World War.

BINNENHOF
THE HAGUE, NETHERLANDS

The Dutch government started using this building in the 1500s and never stopped. It's the oldest continuously used parliament building in the world.

NATIONAL PARLIAMENT HOUSE
DHAKA, BANGLADESH

"Grand" doesn't even describe this enormous and magnificent building. It's considered to be one of the most significant architectural works from the twentieth century.

CAPITOL BUILDINGS
WASHINGTON, D.C., USA

Originally built in 1800, the first US Capitol building quickly proved too small for a growing country. In 1850 it was substantially expanded.

TOOMPEA CASTLE
TALLINN, ESTONIA

Estonia's Parliament meets in an ancient castle that dates back to the ninth century.

PALACE OF THE PARLIAMENT
BUCHAREST, ROMANIA

There's plenty of room to spread out here. This is the largest Parliament building and second-largest office building in the world at 3.7 million square feet—only the Pentagon in the USA is bigger.

WESTMINSTER
LONDON, ENGLAND

The United Kingdom's two main legislative branches, the House of Commons and the House of Lords, both meet at the Palace of Westminster in London, England. In fact, they've been meeting there ever since the 1200s. The original building, built in the eleventh century, burned down in 1512. The new building was also destroyed by fire in 1834. The latest building imitated the medieval Gothic architecture of the one before it. The décor makes it easy to figure out where to go—rooms for the House of Lords are decorated in red, while the House of Commons are in green.

◄ Big Ben

A huge clock and bell tower rises from the walls of the Palace of Westminster. The largest bell is nicknamed Big Ben. The bell cracked in 1859, soon after it went into service, but it is still being used—crack and all.

Next-door Neighbors

Take a short walk out of the Palace of Westminster and you'll end up at another famous British landmark, Westminster Abbey. This 1,000-year-old church is where British kings and queens are crowned.

131

Most Spectacular Canyons

Some are deep, some long, some wide. Some are dry rocks, while others are lush landscapes. Canyons and gorges are like beautiful scars on Earth, showing the amazing history of our planet.

Kali Gandaki Gorge Nepal

Ancient traders who traveled through this Himalayan canyon might have gotten stiff necks from looking up. The canyon runs between two of the world's highest mountains, Dhaulagiri and Annapurna.

Fish River Canyon Nepal

A local story says that a dragon thrashing his tail formed this 100-mile-long canyon. It gets so hot that hikers are only allowed to enter it during a few months out of the year.

Tiger Leaping Gorge China

Any tigers leaping across this gorge had better make it—if not, it's a long fall into the Jinsha River below.

The Verdon Gorge France

Visitors like to kayak on the striking turquoise water of the Verdon River, which formed one of Europe's most beautiful canyons.

ANTELOPE CANYON USA

Flash flooding has eroded the sandstone here to make incredibly smooth rocks that appear to flow like water. The rocks show off the red, gold, yellow, and orange stripes built up by millennia of flooding.

FJAORARGLJUFUR CANYON ICELAND

It's not that long and it's not that deep, but the meandering river, sharp-edged rocks, and greenery make this one of the prettiest canyons around.

COPPER CANYON MEXICO

When copper is exposed to air for a long time, it turns a greenish color (think: old coins or the Statue of Liberty). That's the color of the sides of this canyon, which was formed by six different rivers that cut through it.

COLCA CANYON PERU

One of the deepest canyons in the world, this is home to the majestic Andean condors (wingspan: 10.5 feet) who soar past the cliffsides.

BLYDE RIVER CANYON SOUTH AFRICA

Lots of trees and plants cover these canyon walls. Unlike many of the world's dry and desolate canyons, this one is like a rainforest on the rocks.

GRAND CANYON

The Colorado River has been busy for 17 million years, carving its way through rocks to form the magnificent wonder of the Grand Canyon. It stretches for 277 miles and gets as wide as 18 miles. Its lowest point is 6,093 feet below the rim. Along the way, colorful layers of rock show a geologic history that goes back 2 billion years. Experts think that about half of the depth of the Grand Canyon was formed just in the last 3 million years or so, after the last Ice Age. When glaciers in the Rocky Mountains melted, they caused flash floods. Tremendous amounts of water surged down the mountains. The force of the water carried huge boulders that scraped along the riverbed and made the canyon deeper.

REALLY REMOTE

No cars go to Supai, a village at the bottom of the Grand Canyon where the Havasupai Indians live. Residents and visitors can walk, ride a mule, or take a helicopter. It's the only place in the USA that still has the mail delivered by mule.

◄ GOING IN

In 1869, American explorer John Wesley Powell led a three-month expedition that included the first passage of the Grand Canyon by Europeans.

Highest Mountain Peaks on Each Continent

Each of the seven continents has its own tallest peak. Together, they are called the "Seven Summits." In 1985, mountaineer Richard Bass became the first climber to reach the summits of *all* of them, and that's considered a major achievement for ambitious mountaineers.

7. Puncak Jaya
Australia

Among the Seven Summits, Puncak Jaya is the shortest, but considered the most technically difficult mountain to climb.
Height: 16,024 feet.

6. Mt. Vinson
Antarctica

Located on a cold and unpopulated continent, Mt. Vinson is the most off-the-beaten-path mountain in the world. It's snowy and bitterly cold—but that didn't stop a team from reaching the summit in 1966.
Height: 16,066 feet.

5. Mt. Elbrus
Europe, Russia

Mountaineers who want to climb Mt. Elbrus can hitch a ride part of the way. A cable car system reaches 12,500 feet.
Height: 18,510 feet.

4. Mt. Kilimanjaro
Africa, Tanzania

Mt. Kilimanjaro is actually a volcanic mountain, comprised of three major volcanic peaks. The last eruption was 150,000 to 200,000 years ago.
Height: 19,345 feet.

3. Denali
North America, USA

"Denali" means "the great one" or "the high one." It was named Mt. McKinley in 1896 to support the presidential candidate William McKinley before being changed back to Denali in 2015. Height: 20,237 feet.

2. Aconcagua
South America

Aconcagua is part of the Andes, the longest mountain range in the world. It was first summited in 1897 by Swiss climber Matthias Zurbriggen.
Height: 22,837 feet.

137

1. EVEREST
NEPAL

The crown jewel in mountaineering, the summit of Everest was first reached in 1953 by the New Zealand climber and explorer Sir Edmund Hillary and his Sherpa guide Tenzing Norgay. While Everest is not the most technically difficult mountain to climb, dangers from altitude sickness and bad weather pose constant threats. Once climbers reach the "death zone" (above 26,000 feet), they only have a couple of days in which their bodies can endure the high altitude. If bad weather keeps them from reaching the top quickly, they usually must turn back. Some 4,000 climbers have conquered Everest, but the mountain has taken its toll. Eight climbers died on the mountain in 1996 when they became trapped by a blizzard. In 2015, another 18 were killed by an avalanche that hit the climbers' base camp.

Way Up in Asia

As tall as all those world mountains are, the tallest mountains in the world are all in Asia, clustered together in the Himalaya and Karakoram mountain ranges in Asia. Here are the top five on the world list.

5. Makalu

One of the most difficult mountains in the world to climb, no one reached the top of Makalu during the winter season until 2009.
Height: 27,838 feet.

4. Lhotse

Lhotse is right next door to Everest. In fact, climbers who want to summit Everest from the south must climb part of Lhotse on the way up.
Height: 27,940 feet.

3. Kangchenjunga

To respect local beliefs that the top of Kangchenjunga is reserved for the gods, summiting teams stop short of going to the very top.
Height: 28,169 feet.

2. K2

Talk about risky. One-fourth of climbers who attempt K2 die in the process. The "Savage Mountain" is one of the most difficult to conquer in the world, and it has never been climbed in winter.
Height: 28,251 feet

1. Mt. Everest

Was Mallory First?

Thirty years before Hillary reached the top of Everest, an Englishman named George Mallory tried in 1924. Climbers farther down the mountain last saw him near the summit, before he disappeared into the clouds. He wasn't seen again until 1999, when his body was found. The big question is, did he fall on his way up, or his way back down? To this day there is speculation about whether Mallory was really the first to reach the top of Everest.

WORLD'S TALLEST BUILDINGS

Since the first skyscrapers were built more than a century ago, architects have been in a race to the skies. They all want to build the tallest structures possible. This is a list that has changed often over the decades and is sure to change again as new designs and ways of building are created. Enjoy this list of the world's tallest buildings—just don't look down!

10. KK100
SHENZEN, CHINA
1,449 FEET

If you want the best views of this city near Hong Kong, check into the hotel that is located in the top 20 floors of this enormous building.

9. WILLIS TOWER
CHICAGO, USA
1,451 FEET

At the top of this tower, once the tallest in the USA, is a glass-floored booth that sticks out from the side of the building. Stand on it and pretend you're floating!

8. ZIFENG TOWER
NANJING, CHINA
1,476 FEET

Glass and metal panels on the outside of this building were created to look like the scales of a dragon—one of the creatures in many ancient Chinese myths.

7. Petronas Towers 1 and 2
Kuala Lampur, Malaysia
1,483 feet—each!

Both these buildings are exactly the same and are connected by a bridge at the 41st floor. Different companies built each tower, with a race to see who would finish first. The team from South Korea claimed the prize.

6. International Commerce Center
Hong Kong
1,588 feet

Packed with businesses and people, this very large and tall building has to deal with a lot of trash. To help, 90 percent of the occupants take part in a huge recycling effort.

5. Shanghai World Financial Center
Shanghai, China
1,614 feet

High buildings deal with high winds. This mega Chinese skyscraper has a curved exterior design that helps deflect incoming winds that would otherwise rattle it.

4. Taipei 101
Taipei, Taiwan
1,667 feet

There are eight stacks of eight floors each in this pagoda-like building. The number eight is considered very good luck by Chinese people!

3. One World Trade Center
New York City, USA
1,776 feet

Plans for this building began within months of the terrible destruction of the previous Twin Towers of the World Trade Center in a terrorist attack in 2001. The height was chosen to honor the year of America's birth.

2. Makkah Royal Clock Tower Hotel
Mecca, Saudi Arabia
1,972 feet

The enormous clock faces at the top of this tower are pretty big all by themselves. They measure 141 feet across. Nearly 100 million glass tiles decorate the structure, some of them covered in gold!

On the Drawing Board

Here are some new super-tall buildings that people are either designing or have begun building:

Kingdom Tower:
Another Dubai skyscraper, this is designed to be more than 3,200 feet tall!

Dubai One:
Dubai's airspace is going to be crowded once this 2,333-foot building is finished.

Signature Tower Jakarta:
Indonesia will have its first megabuilding— if they can find the money to build this plan for a 2,093-foot structure.

Rama IX Super Tower:
Soaring over the ancient city of Bangkok, this would be one of eight buildings around the world proposed to top the 2,000-foot mark.

1. BURJ KHALIFA
DUBAI, UNITED ARAB EMIRATES
2,717 FEET

Second place is a long way down from the top of this amazing building. It's more than 700 feet taller than any other building in the world (for now!). That's 70 more stories!

Cool highlights of Burj Khalifa:

- A FOUNTAIN NEAR ITS BASE CAN SHOOT WATER 500 FEET IN THE AIR.

- At.Mosphere, THE WORLD'S HIGHEST RESTAURANT, IS LOCATED ON THE 122ND LEVEL.

- DOUBLE-DECKER ELEVATORS WHOOSH VISITORS TO THE OBSERVATION DECK AT 1,400 FEET. IT IS ALSO THE HIGHEST SUCH DECK IN THE WORLD.

- A DOZEN WINDOW-WASHING MACHINES ARE KEPT IN GARAGES AT VARIOUS LEVELS BEFORE BEING PUT TO USE. BRAVE WORKERS ARE PULLED UP AND DOWN THE SIDES OF THE BUILDING TO CLEAN IT.

LARGEST RAINFORESTS

Insects as large as birds, huge poisonous snakes, the world's tallest trees and strangest fish—all of them call the rainforest home. Rainforests cover only a small percentage of Earth's surface, but most of the world's plant and animal species live there. Rainforests aren't always hot and muggy. Tropical rainforests are hot, but temperate ones are much cooler.

10. DAINTREE RAINFOREST
QUEENSLAND, AUSTRALIA

The descendants of ancient species can still be found in Daintree's 463 square miles. It's home to 90 percent of Australia's bat and butterfly species.

9. TAI NATIONAL PARK COTE D'IVOIRE

Several endangered species, including leopards and chimpanzees, live in the 1,274 square miles of Tai National Park.

8. BOSAWAS BIOSPHERE RESERVE
JINOTEGA, NICARAGUA

Harpy Eagles, the largest species of eagle in the Americas, perch in the treetops of the Bosawas Reserve, which stretches over some 7,700 square miles.

7. CHOCOAN RAINFORESTS
PANAMA, COLUMBIA, AND ECUADOR

The 38,610-mile Choco region is only a few hundred miles from the Amazon, but because the Andes Mountains lie between them, it has unique species that live only here.

6. Valdivian Rainforest
Chile and Argentina, South America

About 18,000 years ago, most of the 95,800 square miles of this temperate rainforest was covered by the Patagonian Ice Sheet.

5. New Guinea Rainforest

The 111,000 square miles of rainforest in New Guinea provide a home for the world's smallest parrot, largest pigeon, and longest lizard.

4. Pacific Temperate Rainforest

This region stretches from California to Alaska, covering 114,000 square miles. The world's tallest tree, the coast redwood, grows here, in just a few places in Northern California.

3. Congo Basin
Africa

About 75 million people live in the 781,000 square miles of the Congo Basin, sharing it with endangered species such as elephants, chimpanzees, and gorillas.

2. Southeast Asia Rainforest

Thousands of years ago, rainforests covered most of the islands that make up Southeast Asia. Now only about half remain. Its 1,112,000 square miles are scattered across the islands.

1. AMAZON RAINFOREST
SOUTH AMERICA

With about 2,100,000 square miles of forest, the Amazon is by far the largest rainforest in the world. It covers most of Brazil and stretches into several other South American countries. The region is home to about ten percent of all the world's species, with 2.5 million different species of insects, 40,000 plants, 2,000 birds and mammals, and 2,000 fish. That's just what scientists have counted so far—they estimate that there are a lot more hiding in the depths of the rainforest.

THE AMAZON RIVER

Binoculars won't help when it comes to looking across the Amazon River. At some points it's several miles wide. During the wet season, the mouth of the river can be 300 miles across. Most of the water from the entire continent of South America drains into the river, which then leads into the Atlantic Ocean. About 500 billion cubic feet of water flow into the ocean every day. That's enough water to supply New York City for nine years! All that water produces a strong current. In fact, freshwater from the Amazon River travels more than 100 miles into the Atlantic before it mixes with saltwater.

Coolest Rain Records

There are lots of ways to measure rain, from how much to how long to how often. Here's a list of some of the coolest world records related to precipitation (that's a fancy way of saying "rain").

Barot Guadeloupe

On November 26, 1970, the residents of Barot, Guadeloupe, saw a record 1.5 inches of rain. Doesn't sound like much? Consider this—it all came in one minute.

Holt Missouri

In 1947, Holt, Missouri, was already experiencing its wettest June for almost 60 years. The evening of June 22 made it even more so, when the town saw 12 inches of rain in 42 minutes.

Shangdi, Nei Monggol China

Shangdi, Nei Monggol, China, wins the record for the most amount of rain in 1 hour, with 15.8 inches on July 3, 1975.

CILAOS RÉUNION

On January 7 and 8, 1966, a 12-hour downpour brought 45 inches of rain to Cilaos, Réunion, an island in the Indian Ocean off the southeast coast of Africa.

. . . And it kept going. Tropical cyclone Denise dumped even more rain on Cilaos over the next 12 hours, bringing the 24-hour total to 71.9 inches.

CHERRAPUNJI INDIA

From August of 1860 to July of 1861, Cherrapunji, India, set the record for the most rain in a one-year period—86.8 feet.

CHERRAPUNJI INDIA

Typically, India's rainy season begins in July, but things got started early in 1995. Two days—June 15 and 16—brought 98.15 inches of rain to Cherrapunji.

CRATERE COMMERSON RÉUNION

Réunion gets a lot of rain! A three-day downpour on February 24, 25, and 26 of 2007 brought 154.72 inches of rain to Cratere Commerson. A further day brought the total to 194.33 inches.

ATACAMA DESERT CHILE

And then there's the other extreme. The Atacama Desert in Chile is the driest place in the world, with less than .004 inches per year. Some places in the desert have had no rain at all in more than 400 years!

MAWSYNRAM INDIA

It's one thing to get a lot of rain in one day or even in one year, but some places keep it up year after year.

Mawsynram, India, takes the prize for the highest average annual rainfall, with 38.95 feet. The rainy monsoon season is even longer and wetter here than in other parts of India. The reason Mawsynram gets so much rain is because of its unique geography. Warm, moist winds traveling north from the Bay of Bengal get stopped by the Khasi Hills. This pushes the air up, cools it down, and makes even more moisture condense out of the clouds—bringing rain directly on to the town of Mawsynram below.

WHEN AN UMBRELLA JUST ISN'T ENOUGH

Living in the world's rainiest place can be challenging. People who work outside often use bamboo and banana leaves to construct wearable, full-body raincoats. And because the constant moisture rots wood, the residents cultivate the roots of rubber trees to grow into waterproof "living bridges" that cross areas that are too wet for wading.

HIGHEST
INHABITED PLACES

Grocery stores? Think again. Internet access? Not so much. The highest inhabited places on Earth are cold and barren, and it's hard to make a living. It's tough times on the top of a mountain, but some people like the peace and quiet.

10. NIAGSU INDIA

Located in the Jammu and Kashmir region in the very north of India, Niagsu is not one of the largest of the region's more than 4,000 towns—but it is one of the highest! Height: 14,921 feet.

9. YELCHANG INDIA

Surrounded by snowy mountains, the tiny settlement of Yelchang is one of India's smallest. If you want to travel to Yelchang, be prepared for a long trip. It's 120 miles from the nearest airport. Height: 14,947 feet.

8. KUSHOL INDIA

In the sparsely populated foothills of the Himalaya Mountain Range, the town of Kushol is recorded at 14,986 feet high. Tourists like to go mountain biking in these hilly regions, but be prepared to pedal a *lot* to get to the top of this town.

7. TAKH INDIA

Also located in the foothills of the Himalayas, the town of Takh sits at the same height as Kushol—14,986 feet.

6. KORZOK INDIA

The ancient village of Korzok is home to the Korzok Monastery. About 70 Tibetan Buddhist monks live in the monastery, which is about 300 years old. Height: 14,995 feet.

5. AMDO TIBET

Known as the "Land of Snows," Amdo is one of Tibet's three main regions. The town of Amdo is its capital, but don't plan a visit—it's closed to tourists. Height: 15,450 feet.

4. YANSHIPING TIBET

Big business hasn't reached Yanshiping. Most residents make their living raising animals. Height: 15,490 feet.

3. LONGREN TIBET

Not many trees or grass can grow at such a high altitude, but there's a little bit in Longren, which provides grazing areas for animals in the region. Height: 15,535 feet.

2. WENQUAN TIBET

Built in 1955 to serve a nearby highway, Wenquan translates to "warm springs." There aren't many of those in a land of snowy mountains, so this is a welcome refuge. Height: 15,980 feet.

1. LA RINCONADA
PERU

The gold mining town of La Rinconada in the Andes mountains, Peru, is the world's highest permanent settlement. It sits at the foot of a glacial mountain named "The Sleeping Beauty." In the first decade of the 2000s, the price of gold skyrocketed—and so did the number of people who moved to La Rinconada, hoping to cash in. It's hard living in La Rinconada, however. For one thing, it's cold, with an average temperature that barely gets above freezing. There is no hotel, no running water, and no sewage system. There is electricity, which is used to transport heavy mining equipment.
Height: 16,700 feet.

Luck of the Draw

The gold miners in La Rinconada are not paid by the hour. In fact, for the first 30 days of their employment they do not make any money at all! On the 31st day, they are allowed to go into the mines for about 4 hours. In that time, they can keep as much rock as they can carry out on their backs. If the rock has gold in it, they could make a fortune. More often, though, it's just a bunch of heavy rocks—and then it's back to the mines to try again.

MOST AMAZING SUNSET VIEWING SPOTS

Happy couples are always walking off into the sunset at the end of romantic movies. But where are the best places to do it? Check out the spectacular scenery at these sunset hot spots!

SUNSET BOULEVARD
USA

The name says it all. At 22 miles long, Sunset Boulevard, California, runs from Downtown Los Angeles all the way west to the Pacific Ocean—a great drive at sunset.

ANGKOR WAT
THAILAND

This complex of Buddhist temples is the world's largest religious monument. It faces west, so the setting sun illuminates its impressive towers.

SVALBARD
NORWAY

On this island in the Arctic Circle, it's so far north that for a period in the summer, the sun doesn't completely set. It just gets lower and lower until it starts going back up again. That means you can watch the sunset for hours!

ISTANBUL
TURKEY

Tall, pointy minarets stand starkly against the setting sun. They are part of Istanbul's many mosques.

The Maldives
Indian Ocean

Hundreds of islands make up this tropical paradise, so there are plenty of beaches to choose from to relax for a spectacular sunset view.

Hawaii
USA

Pick any one of Hawaii's islands to watch the sunset—the Big Island, Maui, or Oahu. Really, it doesn't matter. It's Hawaii!

Key West USA

Every night locals and tourists gather in this part of the Florida Keys for a festival of arts and crafts, performers, and food, and of course to watch the sunset.

Ayers Rock
Australia

The sky turns red at dusk when the sun reflects the red color of Uluru (the Aboriginal name for Ayers Rock), the 1,142-foot tall rock that sits here.

The Matterhorn
Switzerland

The setting sun lights up the tip of this mountain like a giant birthday candle.

Serengeti National Park
Tanzania

It's a sunset safari when graceful giraffes and majestic elephants move across these vast grasslands, creating silhouettes on the horizon.

SANTORINI
GREECE

The island of Santorini is the definition of picturesque. Located in the Aegean Sea off the mainland of Greece, it's got blue waters, steep cliffs, and shining white buildings. When the sun sets, it turns the white buildings to brilliant shades of red, pink, orange, and yellow. Where is the best place to watch from? Either down on the beach, or up high on the cliffs? Maybe the biggest question on a vacation to Santorini is where to set up camp to view the sunset spectacle.

SHAKE IT UP

Santorini was formed by volcanic eruptions millions of years ago, and the volcanoes in this chain of islands are still sometimes active. One of the largest eruptions in history occurred about 3,500 years ago. The Thera eruption led to the downfall of the ancient Minoan civilization and inspired some of Greece's famous myths, such as the civilization of the island of Atlantis.

LARGEST LANDLOCKED COUNTRIES

Going for a day at the beach isn't easy to do for the billions of people who live in landlocked countries. Landlocked means the nations are surrounded by others, with no ocean shoreline. They'll need to find their passports and travel across international borders to get to the sea. The world has almost 200 independent countries, and 43 of them do not border an ocean or sea. There are even a couple of doubly-landlocked nations. They are surrounded by other countries that are also landlocked.

10. CENTRAL AFRICAN REPUBLIC

Located only a few hundred miles from the equator, it gets pretty hot in the CAR. Even though it has no ocean access, most of the country lies within the basin of the large Ubangi River, so swimming is an option—just steer clear of the crocodiles! Size: 240,534 square miles.

9. AFGHANISTAN

With no major waterways to travel on, ancient traders in Afghanistan took to the historic Silk Road, which connected them to Middle Eastern countries where they traded for valuable goods. Size: 251,825 square miles.

8. ZAMBIA

Who needs an ocean? Zambia has some spectacular scenery all on its own. This southern African country is home to Victoria Falls, one of the largest waterfalls in the world. They are a mile wide! Size: 290,586 square miles.

7. BOLIVIA

Bolivia has plenty of highs and lows, ranging from the towering Andes Mountains to the low plains of the Amazon River Basin.
Size: 424,200 square miles.

6. ETHIOPIA

Some 90 million people live within the boundaries of Ethiopia, one of the world's poorest countries. About 80 percent of the population works in agriculture, with livestock and coffee being some of the major exports.
Size: 435,200 square miles.

5. MALI

Mali has plenty of natural resources, including gold, uranium, and salt. But there's not much water. Most of the country is located within the vast Sahara Desert, where rain is scarce.
Size: 478,800 square miles.

4. NIGER

The northern African country of Niger is hot and dry, covered with deserts and semi-deserts. Niger gets its name from the Niger River, but the river's reduced flow threatens the country's water resources.
Size: 489,200 square miles.

3. CHAD

It's a trip of 660 miles to get to the nearest seaport from Chad, located in the center of Africa. A large lake in the western part of the country gives birds and animals a drink and a break from the hot temperatures. Size: 495,800 square miles.

2. MONGOLIA

Bordered by China and Russia, Mongolia is a cold and desolate place. Its ancient nomadic people bred horses to help them travel over rugged mountains and deserts. Size: 604,200 square miles.

MEET THE KAZAKHS!

Centuries ago, nomadic tribes lived in Kazakhstan. The largest of these was the Kazakhs, which is how the country gets its name. Russia took over control of Kazakhstan in the eighteenth century, and the country became part of the Soviet Union in 1936. When the Soviet empire dissolved more than 50 years later, Kazakhstan was on its own again, declaring itself an independent nation.

1. KAZAKHSTAN

Larger than all of Western Europe put together, Kazakhstan is the world's largest landlocked country and the ninth-largest country overall. It does not even fit on one continent! Most of the country is in Asia, but a small part spills into Europe. Despite its large size, Kazakhstan is not densely populated— maybe because it's difficult to travel through the country's steep, snowy mountains and rugged steppes. To reach water, people can travel to the Caspian Sea, which forms part of Kazakhstan's western border. But if there's water, how is it a landlocked country? It's because the Caspian Sea is self-contained. No part of it flows into the ocean. So, it is also considered landlocked.

Size: 1,049,000 square miles.

Most Densely Populated Cities

The people living in one of these large cities share it with 10 million people or more—so they're living as up-close and personal as it gets. At least they don't have to go far if they need to borrow a cup of sugar! Density is a measure of how closely packed things are—in this case it's people!

10. Mexico City Mexico

Founded in the year 325 CE, Mexico City is the oldest capital city in all of the Americas and the largest Spanish-speaking city in the world.
Density: 24,600 people per square mile.

9. Istanbul Turkey

Istanbul was only an informal name for this city formerly known as Constantinople. In 1930, the nation's post office officially changed it.
Density: 25,100 people per square mile.

8. Seoul South Korea

After the Korean War in the 1950s, Seoul turned itself from a poor city into a global power player in a few decades. The 22 million people who live there are considered among the world's most technologically advanced. Density: 27,000 people per square mile.

7. DELHI INDIA

India's capital city is actually a collection of several cities that are bundled together. They've been inhabited for 2,500 years. Density: 29,700 people per square mile.

6. KOLKATA INDIA

Kolkata is next to a large wetlands area. Much of those areas have now been reclaimed—drained and filled in with rock and dirt—to expand the city for its growing population. Density: 30,900 people per square mile.

5. LAGOS NIGERIA

Lagos is Africa's first city and its largest. It's also one of the fastest-growing in the world. Density: 33,000 people per square mile.

4. MANILA
PHILIPPINES

Manila became an important global trading point beginning in the sixteenth century, when goods were shipped across the Pacific Ocean from Manila to ports in Mexico. Density: 39,900 people per square mile.

3. KARACHI PAKISTAN

There are six main languages spoken by the people in Karachi. What language you speak depends on where you live and what you do for a living. Density: 47,300 people per square mile.

2. MUMBAI INDIA

India's largest city is built on a collection of seven islands on the country's western shore. Early residents were mostly fishermen, but today Mumbai is one of the world's most important economic centers. Density: 80,100 people per square mile.

1. DHAKA
BANGLADESH

No place even comes close to Dhaka for most densely populated. Its 15,414,000 people are squeezed into 134 square miles, which averages out to about 115,000 people per square mile. It's even more crowded in the slums, where much of the city's poor population lives. Those areas house as many as 2.7 million people in one square mile. At that density, the world's entire population—6 billion people—could fit in an area a little smaller than the state of Delaware in the USA.

WHAT'S IN A NAME?

No one seems to be sure where Dhaka got its name. It could have come from the dhak tree, which used to be common in the area, or from the musical instrument dhak, which is used in traditional ceremonies. Another theory is that it's a shortened form of Dhakeshwari, a goddess in the Hindu religion who has a temple in the city.

GETTING AROUND

Called the "Rickshaw Capital of the World," Dhaka has hundreds of thousands of these three-wheeled bicycle taxis to transport people around the city. Prettier rickshaws attract more clients, so there's a market for rickshaw painters, as well as pedalers!

Busiest Subways

The traffic is usually bad in the world's busiest cities, so commuters there often prefer to take public transport, which is usually much faster. Subways are older than you might think—the world's first subway system opened in London in 1863. Since then, subways have gotten lots of upgrades. Some have carpets, artwork, and Wi-Fi.

10. Paris
France

Built in 1900, the Paris Metro has lent its name to subway systems all over the world. The word "metro" is short for "metropolitan," which means related to a city.
Annual ridership: 1.54 billion.

9. Hong Kong
China

Opened in 1979, the Hong Kong subway system is one of the most profitable in the world.
Annual ridership: 1.6 billion.

8. Mexico City
Mexico

Think of it as a mini-museum. At some subway stations in Mexico City, passengers can view archaeological artifacts from the country's ancient Aztec and Mayan civilizations.
Annual ridership: 1.69 billion.

7. New York
USA

There are a lot of places to visit in New York City, and chances are there's a nearby subway stop. With 468 stations (so far!), New York has the most of any subway system in the world.
Annual ridership: 1.71 billion.

6. GUANGZHOU
CHINA

The third-largest city in China did not get a subway until 1997, but people quickly got on board with the idea. Annual ridership: 2.05 billion.

5. MOSCOW
RUSSIA

Subway stations in Moscow are often considered the most beautiful in the world, with high, decorated ceilings and chandeliers. Some trains are decorated with copies of famous pieces of art. Annual ridership: 2.49 billion.

4. SHANGHAI
CHINA

The largest city in China first got a subway system in 1995, and it keeps getting bigger. It's one of the fastest-growing subway systems in the world. Annual ridership: 2.5 billion.

3. SEOUL
SOUTH KOREA

It would take a while to take a complete tour of Seoul by subway. It's the longest in the world, with 584 miles of track. Annual ridership: 2.62 billion.

2. BEIJING
CHINA

When Beijing was named as the host city for the 2008 Summer Olympic Games, it expanded its subway system dramatically to handle all the tourists. Annual ridership: 3.21 billion.

1. TOKYO
JAPAN

The first metro line in Tokyo opened in 1927, and it's been growing ever since. About half of Tokyo's commuters choose to ride the subway instead of driving, cycling, or walking. All those people means riding the subway can be a challenge—especially during rush hour. Sometimes people are crowded in so tightly that their feet do not even touch the ground. Employees called "pushers" ensure that everyone is inside the train before the doors close. Despite the mass of people, Tokyo's subway is famous for being orderly, efficient, and clean. When there's enough room, it's common to see people sleeping during their long commutes.
Annual ridership: 3.3 billion.

STRANDED

In March 2011, a powerful 8.9-magnitude earthquake originated off the coast of Japan. It was the strongest earthquake in Japan's recorded history and triggered a massive tsunami. The quake forced the city of Tokyo to shut down the subway system for several hours. Many of the eight million people who depended on the subway were stranded far from home. Three years later, the subways stopped again, as a show of respect for those who died in the earthquake.

ALWAYS MOVING

Tokyo also hosts the busiest individual subway station in the world. The Shinjuku station sees some 3.5 million passengers every day.

BEAUTIFUL BEACHES

When most people think of the perfect vacation spot, they think of a beach. Beaches are often on the lists of the most beautiful places in the world. What makes a beach beautiful? Lots of sunshine, clear waters offshore, lush vegetation, and no crowds of course! Whole books have been created about this topic, so we've just highlighted a few from around the world. Don't forget your sunscreen!

MATIRA BEACH
BORA BORA

The South Pacific islands each offer stunning beaches. Everyone has their favorites, but many experts point to this white sandy stretch. It's on the southern tip of Bora Bora, with aqua blue water and even a coral reef for snorkeling.

EL CASTILLO
TULUM, MEXICO

It's got sand, sun, surf . . . and a towering Mayan ruin! Experience paradise and history at the same time as you frolic in the waves.

HONOKALANI
MAUI, HAWAII

Each of the Hawaiian islands could claim a spot on this list. They all have palm-tree-shaded beaches with warm, tropical waters. This beach on Maui's east coast, however, stands out for its black sand! It was created by wave action pounding on the volcanic rock of the island.

BLINKY BEACH
LORD HOWE ISLAND, AUSTRALIA

It's a long trip to this tiny island off Australia's east coast. Once there, however, clear blue waters and perfect surf make the journey worth it!

ANSE SOURCE D'ARGENT
SEYCHELLES

You've probably seen pictures of this beach in ads for many products. The models have to travel a long way to reach these islands in the Indian Ocean. Once there, they can enjoy amazing weather, unique sea life, and perfect blue water.

EAST BEACH
SANTA BARBARA, CALIFORNIA

Play volleyball, eat great pancakes, get some sun, and then watch the twinkling lights at night on the low hills behind you. East Beach is one of the most famous beach volleyball sites in the USA and is located in a great resort town ideal for family visits.

CAPE COD BAY

Cape Cod sticks out like a curved arm from Massachusetts. The inner curve of the arm is lined with beach after beach. The unique part of this site, however, comes when the tide goes out. Much of the inner Bay becomes a huge, soggy, sand-bar-covered "beach" that stretches for a couple of miles. People love to walk in with the tide as the beach "disappears."

SEVEN MILE BEACH
JAMAICA

Miles of white beach and acres of palm trees, huts for shade, or hotels for sleeping. Horse rides, snorkeling, or just snoozing. All that, plus this beach faces west, so it boasts some of the most spectacular sunsets in the world.

PINK SANDS,
THE BAHAMAS

Beach lovers will each put their own favorite sandy spot on the top of this list, but we're picking this wide and empty spot for one big reason—it has beautiful pink sand. On the Atlantic side of the central Bahamas, Pink Sands stretches for miles with nothing but pink sand. Palm trees line the land side, while Gulf Stream waters lap easily on the shore. The beach is on Harbour Island, east of the main body of Bahamas islands.

So why is it pink? Most sand is made up from minerals and rocks that have been pounded over the years into tiny grains. However, much of the material that formed Pink Sands comes from animals, not minerals. Marine animals called foraminifera have red or pink shells on their tiny, tiny bodies. After they die the shells collect in the water and are deposited on the beach. The animals live in great numbers in the waters off of what become pink sand beaches like this one. Other pink sand beaches can be found in Greece, the Philippines, and Caribbean islands near the Bahamas.

HAPPIEST COUNTRIES

It may not be possible to buy happiness, but money doesn't hurt either, according to the World Happiness Report. It studied countries all over the world, looking at factors such as income, employment opportunities, living standards, health, and perceptions of freedom. So who's happiest? Take a look!

10. AUSTRALIA

With beautiful beaches, warm temperatures, and the amazing Great Barrier Reef, Australia is a popular tourist destination. Apparently its residents love it, too.

9. NEW ZEALAND

This island is full of natural wonders and lies southwest of its also-happy neighbor, Australia.

8. SWEDEN

Even though 15 percent of Sweden lies north of the Arctic Circle, most of the country experiences moderate temperatures and distinct seasons.

7. THE NETHERLANDS (HOLLAND)

Windmills and colorful fields of tulips are common in the Netherlands, which is extremely flat—only half of it rises more than 3.3 feet above sea level.

6. FINLAND

Finland was the first nation in the world to grant all adult citizens both the right to vote and to run for office.

5. CANADA

British and French settlers came to Canada in the 1400s, and the country still has two official languages—English and French.

4. NORWAY

Need a friend? Pick a Norwegian. Ninety-five percent of them said they had someone they could count on if they needed it.

3. DENMARK

Why are Danes so happy? Perhaps it's their belief in the idea of *hygge*— enjoying life with friends and family.

2. ICELAND

Iceland has been rated the most peaceful nation on Earth, perhaps proving that peace is a key to happiness.

1. SWITZERLAND

Healthy, wealthy, and wise—the Swiss really do have it all! Swiss citizens have a high average income and are power players in the world's economy. They live on average for a long time, and when countries need a dispute settled, there's no country like Switzerland to get the peace process rolling. They've also got great chocolate! Medical studies show that countries whose residents eat a lot of chocolate tend to produce more citizens who win Nobel prizes (an international award given in various fields). Switzerland has produced a lot of Nobel prize winners, including the famous physicist Albert Einstein, who was living in the Swiss city of Bern when he developed the theory of relativity.

MATTERHORN

Disneyland claims to be the "happiest place on Earth," but it's taken a cue from Switzerland, too. One of its oldest and most beloved attractions is the roller coaster ride known as the Matterhorn, which is based on a mountain in the Swiss Alps.

WHEN THE KITCHEN MEETS THE MAP

BRUSSELS SPROUTS take their name from the capital of Belgium. They were not originally from that country, however. They got the name in the 1600s.

Next time you're looking for something to eat, instead of getting out a restaurant menu or looking in the fridge, get out your atlas! Hundreds of types of food are named after real places around the world. If this list doesn't make you hungry, we don't know what will!

Ever wondered how you copy a taste? After returning from India, Lord Sandys of England hired a pair of chemists to re-make a sauce he had tried during his travels. They were eventually successful, and the spicy mix took its name from Lord Sandys home county of Worcester— **WORCESTERSHIRE SAUCE!**

The history of the name for **BRUNSWICK STEW** is disputed. Cities with that name in both Virginia and Georgia claim to be the original home of the meaty mixture. Southern towns often make huge pots of it for fundraising community dinners.

Clam chowder fans divide into two camps. White and creamy **NEW ENGLAND CHOWDER** is the older, more popular version. A tomato-based clam chowder from early in the twentieth century is known as **MANHATTAN CHOWDER.**

SARDINES are small fish that swim in huge schools. There are many species of fish commonly called sardines; most are part of the herring family. The name probably comes from the Italian island of Sardinia.

The first **ECCLES CAKES** were sold, not surprisingly, in Eccles, a town in central England near Manchester. A store owned by a baker named James Birch helped spread the raisin-filled treats around.

TABASCO SAUCE was named by its inventor, who never actually went to Tabasco, Mexico. Edmund McIlhenny started making the spicy stuff in Louisiana in the 1860s.

The most famous home of the big and crunchy **VIRGINIA PEANUT** is right there in its name, but they are also grown in other southeastern states.

ON THE OTHER HAND...

Instead of food being named for places, here are a few towns in the USA named for food!
Cookietown, Oklahoma
Chicken, Arkansas

Tortilla Flat, Arizona
Two Egg, Florida
Pie Town, New Mexico
Spuds, Florida
Strawberry, California

A WORLD OF CHEESE

Cheese is one of the oldest foods known to humans. It has been made all over the world for thousands of years. An archaeologist found evidence of cheese-making on 7,500-year-old pottery dug up in Poland. Each village, town, or region developed its own kind of cheese, made from the milk of cows, goats, or sheep. Different flavors, different cheese-making methods, and different local tastes have created a real world of cheese. Here's a tour of some of the most famous international homes of great cheese!

FRANCE

For hundreds of years, France was a very rural country. As in many European nations, cheese was made in small batches in village after village. Many of them have become staple parts of the French diet and are known worldwide. Famous cheeses: Brie, Camembert, Roquefort, Munster.

UNITED KINGDOM

You can tell if a cheese is from Great Britain if its name is on a British map. More than 700 cheeses originated in the British Isles and have spread around the world. Every county had farmers that made cheese with local milk, creating a tapestry of cheese types and flavors. Famous cheeses: Cheddar, Stilton, Cheshire, Double Gloucester, Red Leicester, Wensleydale, and many more.

SPAIN

Spain is a pretty big country, so what kind of cheese you eat depends on where you are when you eat it. Cheese is often part of Spanish dishes, or eaten alone with wine. Famous cheeses: Manchego, Zamorano, Mahón, San Simon.

ITALY

You can't really have a great Italian meal without cheese in there somewhere. Whether it's melted in lasagna, gooey in ravioli, or sprinkled over spaghetti, it's been part of Italian diets for years. And that's not even mentioning pizza! Famous cheeses: Ricotta, Parmesan, Mozzarella, Provolone, Asiago.

USA

World cheese experts turn their noses up at what is called American cheese, the yellow/orange stuff found on sandwiches everywhere. But great cheeses do come from America—many from the dairies of the upper Midwest. A third of the milk produced by Amerian cows is turned into cheese of one sort or another. Note that Velveeta in a spray can is not really cheese! Most of the recipes used to make cheese in America came from somewhere else around the world. Famous cheeses: Jack cheese.

SWITZERLAND

Most of the land in this European country can't be farmed, but it is good for growing grass. And cows love grass. So that means lots of cows, lots of milk, ... and lots of cheese! More than 450 types of cheese are produced here, including some using milk from goats or sheep. Famous names: Emmentaler, Gruyère, Sbrinz.

World's Busiest Airports

If you go to one of the airports on this list, you will not be alone! Airports are the landing spots for the hundreds of thousands of flights that take people around the world every year. Airports keep track of how many people visit, and it's always an interesting list. These are the busiest airports in the world. Some attract many people who stay in those cities, while others are more often places where people catch connecting flights!

10. Hong Kong (HKG)
63.1 million

Open since 1998, this busy airport is built on a man-made island in Hong Kong Harbor. Its location in southern China makes it a central hub for Asian flights.

9. Dallas/Fort Worth, Texas (DFW)
63.5 million

With a location in the middle of the busy USA airline map, DFW is one of the busiest connection hubs. That's airline speak for where many of their flights take off and land.

8. Paris, France (CDG)
63.8 million

This is Charles de Gaulle Airport—one of three that serve the French capital. The city is always high on the list of the most popular tourist spots . . . and most people fly there!

7. Chicago, Illinois (ORD)
69.9 Million

How important is Chicago's O'Hare Airport? When bad weather hits the area, flights all across the USA and even the world are delayed. Thousands of flights connect in this central location every day.

5. Los Angeles, California (LAX)
70.6 Million

Just say "LAX" if you're aiming for this West Coast location. It's one of the few airports whose official three-letter call sign is well-known by the general public.

3. London, England (LHR)
73.4 Million

Heathrow Airport is by far the busiest around this important world capital, but fliers can also choose London City or Gatwick Airports.

6. Dubai, United Arab Emirates (DXB)
70.4 Million

This is the busiest airport in the world in terms of international passengers. It took over the top spot in 2014, a sign of the growing power of this small Middle Eastern nation.

4. Tokyo, Japan (HND)
72.8 Million

This might be a large number, but Tokyo also has Narita Airport, which brings in tens of millions of passengers each year.

2. Beijing, China (PEK)
86.1 Million

It's now Beijing Capital International Airport, but for many years, this city was called Peking . . . which explains how it got its three-letter name from international air authorities.

Airport Code Quiz

Which of the following are real airport codes, and which are made up?

OGG	WOW
PEE	GNU
BAD	BOO
EEK	HOT

(answer: It's a trick: They're all real!)

1. ATLANTA
GEORGIA (ATL)

The busiest airport in the world is Hartsfield–Jackson International in Atlanta, Georgia. Atlanta is a great place to visit, but only a small fraction of the 96.1 million people who land in Atlanta actually leave the airport to see the Peach City. That's because Atlanta is one of the most important "hubs" in the system of airline routes. To make sure that people can get to all the places they want to go, airlines created this system, which looks like a bike wheel. Hubs like Atlanta are at the center, with the many spokes going out from there to dozens of other cities. By making many of the connections between flights in one place, airlines can keep costs down, control where planes are, and coordinate schedules with other airlines. The airport in Atlanta has been the world's busiest since 1998. Delta Airlines is by far the biggest airline serving Atlanta, but dozens of other carriers fly there, too.

WHERE'D THEY GET THE NAME?

William Hartsfield was an Atlanta mayor who was a driving force behind building the city's first airport in the 1920s. Maynard Jackson was the city's mayor three times. The airport took on the Hartsfield name in 1980 and added Jackson in 2003 after his death.

Atlanta
Air

WORLD'S LARGEST AIRPORTS BY SIZE

Another way to rank airports is by physical size. These sprawling facilities are the largest in the world in terms of area.

1. KING FAHD INTERNATIONAL AIRPORT, SAUDI ARABIA. ONE OF ITS FOUR TERMINALS IS RESERVED FOR USE BY THE SAUDI ROYAL FAMILY.
2. DENVER (COLORADO) INTERNATIONAL AIRPORT
3. DALLAS/FORT WORTH INTERNATIONAL AIRPORT
4. SHANGHAI PUDONG INTERNATIONAL AIRPORT
5. CHARLES DE GAULLE AIRPORT (PARIS)

TAKE A HIKE!

Taking a hike is a great way to see nature up close, plus they can take you to places with beautiful views. We spend most of our time in cars or trains or airplanes, and we're missing out on some of the world's most amazing and spectacular places. For these hikes, you don't need to be a mountain goat or a Scout, just a person with time on their hands (and some good shoes!). Many of these hikes are not that remote and can be attempted by anyone who is in pretty good shape. Why not go find a hike near you?

THE NARROWS
ZION NATIONAL PARK, USA

It's worth a trip to southern Utah just for this popular walk. Splash through a creek that cuts into tall cliff faces. Pick the right time of year, though, as the river can rise quickly.

SENTIERO AZZURRO
CINQUE TERRE, ITALY

Walk from town to town on a thin walkway along the northwest coast of Italy. Wooden walkways mix with dirt paths, all with amazing views of the blue water and green hills.

APPALACHIAN TRAIL
USA

You can't do this in a day . . . or a week, but you can dip into parts of it from Maine to Georgia. The trail roughly follows the Appalachian Mountains for more than 2,000 miles, taking walkers through a variety of rural and forest areas.

Coast to Coast Walk
Auckland, New Zealand

Auckland is split by an isthmus—a narrow piece of land bounded by water. This hike takes you across the land, from one body of water to another. Pass by volcanoes (they're inactive!) and city parks as you go.

Lions Rock
Hong Kong

The walk is a bit steep, but the view is amazing. The cityscape of Hong Kong spreads out below you, with Hong Kong Bay in the background.

El Caminito del Rey Spain

This is another long trail that you can do in parts. It began as a pilgrimage trail to a holy city in Spain, Santiago. Today, it is in Spain and partly in France and includes many small cities and hostels along its 400-plus miles.

Kalalau Trail
Kauai, Hawaii

Just past the little town of Hanalei on Kauai's North Shore, you can dive into rainforest splendor on this trail. It hugs the high cliffs above some of the most beautiful and unspoiled beaches in the world

Bibbulmun Track
Australia

Hike through forests, valleys, and more near Australia's southwestern coast. This well-maintained and well-marked trail comes in many sections along its 620-mile route. Campsites, shelters, and even comfortable inns are available for walkers.

Franconia Ridge Loop New Hampshire

Walk on the ridges of several mountains on this day-long loop in the White Mountains. Get amazing views off both sides of the trail, which does have some steeper parts and is about 5,000 feet in elevation at points.

Solomon Gulch Trail Valdez, Alaska

This is one of many short trails near Valdez that let visitors get a taste of amazing Alaskan scenery without going into the backcountry. Walk by lakes and beneath towering, snow-covered mountains, and even skirt gravel beaches along Alaska's southern coast.

TOUR DU MONT BLANC

Three countries, more than 100 miles, and everything from mountains and glaciers to meadows and ancient buildings—that's what you'll find on this very popular hike in Europe. The trail circles Mont Blanc, one of the tallest peaks in the Alps. It includes stretches in France, Italy, and Switzerland, although hikers can just enjoy shorter sections in one of those countries if they prefer!

series of huts and hostels as well as small villages d towns adds some local flavor (and places to eat d sleep!) along the way. Backpackers love this route, ough they do have to climb up some steep sections. e hike climbs as much as 10,000 feet during the ll route.

The views are spectacular, but there is also a lot to see close-up, including wildflower displays and animals such as eagles and deer.

For Bolder Hikers

One of the most famous hikes in the world is up a mountain, not around it. Africa's highest peak is Mt. Kilimanjaro between Kenya and Tanzania. Thousands of people have made the 5–9 day walk up its sides. However, many people have had to turn back due to the altitude. But if you're very hardy and up for a climb, it's an amazing view from the top!

Biggest Craters

Sometimes the Earth is just in the wrong place at the wrong time. Falling meteorites and asteroids have come fast, hit hard, and left some really big holes behind. The evidence is still here—millions of years later.

10. Kara Crater
Yugorsky Peninsula, Russia

When a meteor first hit the Earth 70 million years ago, it probably made a hole 75 miles wide. It's shrunk since then. Now it's only 40 miles across.

8. Puchezh-Katunki Crater
Chkalousky District, Russia

Large, crashing meteors usually spell problems for life on Earth, but scientists think this impact did not cause any species to become extinct. Diameter: 50 miles.

9. Morokweng Crater
Kalahari Desert, South Africa

When scientists drilled deep into this crater, they found a 10-inch fragment of the original meteorite that made it 145 million years ago. Diameter: 44 miles.

7. Chesapeake Bay Crater
Virginia, USA

The rounded shape of the west side of Chesapeake Bay comes from a comet or asteroid that hit just off the coast some 35 million years ago. Diameter: 53 miles.

6. Acraman Crater
South Australia

A shallow salt lake now covers the bottom of this 580-million-year-old crater. Scientists found debris from the impact that had fallen 185 miles away.
Diameter: 56 miles.

5. Manicouagan Crater
Quebec, Canada

An asteroid about 3 miles across was responsible for making this crater 215 million years ago. The crater has since been turned into a reservoir.
Diameter: 62 miles.

4. Popigai Crater
Siberia, Russia

It's like an underground jewelry store that's been in business for 35 million years. When a meteorite hit, the force of the impact pressurized the underground carbon reserves and turned them into diamonds.
Diameter: 62 miles.

3. Chicxulub Crater
Yucatan Peninsula, Mexico

It was one killer meteor that made this hole 65 million years ago. Scientists believe the impact upset the environment so much that it led to the extinction of dinosaurs.
Diameter: 110 miles.

2. Sudbury Crater
Ontario, Canada

Fragments of debris from this impact have been found across the country's border in Montana, about 500 miles away.
Diameter: 120 miles.

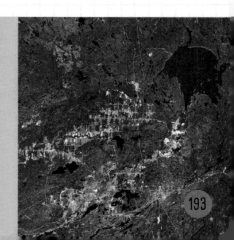

1. VREDEFORT CRATER
SOUTH AFRICA

More than 2 billion years old, Vredefort is one of the Earth's oldest known craters—and the largest. Researchers estimate that it formed when an asteroid three to six miles across plummeted into the ground at 93,200 miles per hour. The impact was the single largest release of energy in Earth's history. Originally the crater was about 190 miles across, but not much is left now. It has mostly eroded. Most of what remains is in the smaller Vredefort Dome, located in the middle of the crater. The site contains lots of important geological information about how the Earth formed. In 2005, the United Nations Educational, Scientific and Cultural Organization (UNESCO) added the crater to its list of world heritage sites.

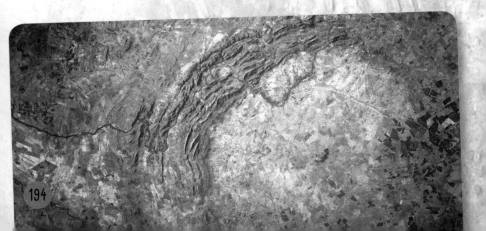

ORIGINAL CRATER RIM

VREDEFORT DOME

Even the largest craters on Earth don't compare to one on the moon. The moon's South Pole-Aitken crater is about 1,600 miles across and is one of the largest in the solar system. It's been around for about four billion years. The crater is not visible from Earth, but lunar explorations in the 1960s showed scientists it existed.

AMAZING NATIONAL PARKS

Until 1872, the idea of a nation setting aside land for a national park was unheard of. But thanks to early environmentalists such as John Muir, the USA made Yellowstone the first official national park. This meant that the amazing beauty of that area would be preserved forever. In the decades since, more than 7,000 natural areas around the world have been named as national parks. Thanks to this sort of vision, these unspoiled and beautiful places will be around for your grandchildren's grandchildren to see!

FJORDLAND NATIONAL PARK
NEW ZEALAND

Have you seen the Lord of the Rings movie? Much of it was filmed in the majestic mountains of this park. Waterfalls, huge lakes, tall peaks, and more have turned it into a sightseer's dream on this nation's South Island.

TIKAL NATIONAL PARK GUATEMALA

This park celebrates not only nature, but history. The park is in a vast forest with wetlands and some amazing creatures. But it also surrounds the remains of an ancient Mayan city that dates back more than 2,000 years.

IGUAZU FALLS
ARGENTINA

Niagra Falls is a trickle compared to this onslaught of falling water. The falls span more than 1.6 miles across, thundering from a high plateau into the rivers below. More than a million people visit the park facilities to get close-up views of this wonder of the world.

SERENGETI NATIONAL PARK
TANZANIA

Nothing says Africa like a safari, and almost nowhere is better for seeing animals in their habitats than this huge, flat park. The Serengeti is the crossroads for millions of animals that migrate each year. The park preserves the area from hunters and civilization.

KAKADU NATIONAL PARK AUSTRALIA

The vast Australian desert is one of the most remote and beautiful places on Earth. Part of it is preserved here, including land on which native people called Aboriginal and Torres Strait Islander peoples have lived for more than 50,000 years. See cave paintings amid spectacular desert scenery.

BANFF NATIONAL PARK CANADA

Canada jumped on the national park bandwagon in 1885 when it established this vast western area for preservation. Outdoor adventurers love the great hikes, raging rivers, quiet lakes, wildflower fields, and snow glaciers of this diverse area.

RAPA NUI NATIONAL PARK

You know it better as Easter Island. Owned by Chile, this entire tiny island is a national park now. It is home to the mysterious giant carved stone heads known as Rapa Nui to the natives. No one really knows how they got there or who made them, but they still stand today, thousands of years later.

Fuji-Hakone-Izu National Park Japan

Talk about diverse! This huge park in Japan includes its most famous single site, the white cone of Mt. Fuji. It also includes the coastline around the Izuhanto peninsula, plus the Izu islands off the coast. That's not to mention the Hakone volcanic region, with its steaming landscape.

Galápagos National Park
Ecuador

The islands of the Galápagos have been protected as one of the most unique places for wildlife in the world. The great scientist Charles Darwin wrote down how evolution works after visiting this isolated spot. Visitors can see iguanas, tortoises, birds, and some stark but beautiful scenery.

Göreme National Park Turkey

They call the spiky rock formations here "chimneys," but they are not for fires. The cones in this park in Turkey were formed by erosion, but also used to be home to thousands of people who carved out caves and homes in the rocks. A popular way to see the site is by hot-air balloon!

Most Popular National Parks in the USA

1. **Great Smoky Mountains National Park** (Tennessee, North Carolina)
2. **Grand Canyon National Park** (Arizona)
3. **Yosemite National Park** (California)
4. **Yellowstone National Park** (Wyoming, Montana, Idaho)
5. **Rocky Mountain National Park** (Colorado)

Ansel Adams

Ansel Adams was one of the world's most famous photographers. His favorite subjects were Yosemite and Yellowstone. He worked in black-and-white, but his images of the vistas of national parks helped draw millions to see them in person.

YELLOWSTONE
NATIONAL PARK

The world's first remains one of the world's best. Yellowstone was formed as the first National Park in 1872 to preserve its unique and beautiful landscape. It includes parts of Wyoming, Montana, and Idaho and takes in mountains, lakes, meadows, hot springs, and more. Visitors to the park come from around the world to marvel at the scenery and to see the park's many animals. It is home to one of the largest remaining herds of bison, which once roamed the West in the millions.

One of Yellowstone's most unique features comes from underground. The park includes one of the world's biggest concentrations of geysers. These are jets of hot water from deep in Earth that shoot out through holes in the ground. The most famous, Old Faithful, erupts every 30–90 minutes. Other hot spots include the Grand Prismatic Spring. Colored minerals make this hot spring one of the most photographed places in the park.

Most Damaging STORMS

When the mighty winds of a powerful storm meet buildings, trees, and bridges . . . the storm wins every time. Add to that the massive flow of ocean water that can be pushed onto the land, plus high rainfall, and you've got a recipe for disaster. In the Atlantic and Pacific Oceans near the USA, such storms are called hurricanes. If they hit in Asia and the western Pacific, they are called typhoons. And in Southeast Asia or the South Pacific, it is called a cyclone. No matter what you call this type of storm, they are deadly. Here are ten twentieth-century storms that were among the deadliest weather events.

10. Hurricane Andrew
1992, 65 deaths

Before Andrew, hurricanes had done a lot of property damage to be sure. After Andrew, there was a new record, unfortunately. Crossing a heavily populated area with Category 5 winds, Andrew wiped out more than 120,000 homes. The damage estimate topped $26 billion. Amazingly, it could have been worse had the storm hit Miami just to the south.

9. Hurricane Camille
1969, 250 deaths

How fast were the winds? No one knows. All the gear that could have measured the wind as this storm hit the Mississippi Gulf coast was smashed by that very same wind. More than 250 people died as a result of the storm or the flooding it caused in far-off Virginia.

8. MIAMI HURRICANE
1926, 372 DEATHS

Many of the deaths occurred when people new to Florida came out of their shelters as the calm eye of the hurricane passed over the city. When the high winds returned, they were caught amid flying debris and a 10-foot storm surge that swept over Miami Beach.

6. GALVESTON HURRICANE
1900, 12,000 DEATHS

As many as 12,000 people died in the winds, flooding, and rain that crushed southern Texas. Massive waves driven by the storm crashed over the beaches and wharves of Galveston. As the water rushed into city streets, people were pulled from their destroyed homes, and many drowned.

7. HURRICANE KATRINA

HURRICANE KATRINA 2005, 1,577 DEATHS IN LOUISIANA, 200 IN MISSISSIPPI

This damaging hurricane blew through the crowded city of New Orleans. Huge levees designed to protect the city failed as the storm surge was bigger than expected. Tens of thousands of people were left stranded or homeless. Entire neighborhoods were underwater. The Louisiana Superdome sports stadium became a last refuge for thousands of people. In many ways, the city is still recovering from this awful storm.

◄ Bridge damage near Biloxi, Mississippi, caused by Hurricane Katrina in 2005.

► A wrecked shrimp trawler boat grounded in Louisiana in the aftermath of Hurricane Katrina.

► Several more grounded shrimp boats.

5. Swatow, China
1922, 100,000 (est.) deaths

This city is now known as Shantou, and it stands at the mouth of the Rongjiang River in southwestern China. A huge storm surge pushed up the river, causing flooding at the harbor and at towns farther from the sea.

3. Cyclone 02B, Bangladesh
1991, 138,866 deaths

A massive storm surge swept Pacific Ocean water across Bangladesh. Even the lessons from the 1970 disaster (see entry below) were not enough for people to have found shelter.

4. Cyclone Nargis, Myanmar
1922, 138,366 deaths

This is the official total, but it could very well be much, much higher. Officials of the country, then known as Burma, did not let many outsiders in to help. Some estimates think as many as five times that number of people might have died.

2. Super Typhoon Nina, China
1975, 171,000 deaths

Two collapsing dams played a big part in the flooding that followed this storm, which brought rainfall of 7.5 inches per hour at one point!

1. Great Bhola Cyclone, Bangladesh
1970, 300,000–500,000 deaths

A combination of low-lying land, crowded conditions, and poor communication proved deadly. This mighty storm struck at night when many people—including tens of thousands living in tightly-packed cities and towns—were asleep. A storm surge rolled across a large part of the country, catching many people in its grip. Almost nine out of ten homes in the disaster area were destroyed, and more than half of the area's fishermen were killed when caught in their boats by the storm. In the aftermath of the government's poor job of helping people, a liberation movement was started, and the new nation of Bangladesh was formed out of what was at the time East Pakistan.

COUNTRIES THAT STILL HAVE A KING OR QUEEN

Here's a look around the world at countries that still have a king or a queen (or other similar royalty) as part of their system of government. Each country's royalty has its own part to play. In some places, they still make all the rules, but in most, they are ceremonial and symbolic links to the past.

10. TONGA
KING TUPOU VI

The newest member of this list, he took over the job in the summer of 2015. Toughest job in Tonga? The royal barber—it's against Tongan law for anyone to touch the head of the king!

9. OMAN
SULTAN QABOOS BIN SAID

This sultan has been in charge of a Middle Eastern country longer than anyone. His rule traces back to the 1600s, when Oman was formed. He is aging, however, and it's a bit of a mystery as to who will follow him, as he has no sons.

8. NORWAY
KING HARALD V

Born in 1937, Harald is one of the oldest monarchs in Europe. Next up for Norway after Harald moves on? His oldest son, Crown Prince Haakon.

7. SPAIN
KING FELIPE VI

Felipe took over in 2014 after an unusual move by his dad, King Juan Carlos. The older king decided to retire—if you're a monarch, that means you stand down to let your son or daughter take over.

6. LIECHTENSTEIN
PRINCE HANS-ADAM II

Like many monarchs, Hans-Adam is not just a prince. His business card would have to read "Prince Hans-Adam II of Liechtenstein, Duke of Troppau and Jägerndorf, Count of Rietberg, Reigning Prince of the House of Liechtenstein." Whew!

5. LESOTHO
KING LETSIE III

Lesotho is a landlocked nation inside South Africa. Letsie actually took turns with his father, King Moshoeshoe, as monarch, before taking over permanently in 1996.

4. CAMBODIA
KING NORODOM SIHAMONI

As a young man, Sihamoni excelled in the arts, becoming a dance professor in Paris, among other places. Since taking over as king in 2004, he has been rather quiet and dignified, very different from his politically-minded father.

2. BHUTAN
KING JIGME KHESAR NAMGYEL

Like his father before him, King Jigme has helped move his nation from a straight monarchy to one that elects its leaders. They kept the king's job, however, and Jingme is the fifth "Dragon King." Born in 1980, he is one of the youngest monarchs in the world.

3. BAHRAIN
KING HAMAD IBN ISA

This tiny Middle Eastern nation has been run by this king since 2002. His previous title was emir, another royal post. His family has run Bahrain since 1783.

1. THE UNITED KINGDOM AND NORTHERN IRELAND
QUEEN ELIZABETH II

A woman named Elizabeth Windsor got a new important job in 1952 . . . and as of 2015, she is still doing it. She took the title of Queen Elizabeth II and has since been the British monarch longer than anyone in history. And that's a pretty long history! The list of British monarchs begins with Egbert way back in 827 CE—around 1,200 years ago!

Elizabeth took over following the death of her father, King George VI. She was actually traveling in Kenya at the time. She and her husband, Prince Philip, returned for the coronation ceremony in London.

Queen Elizabeth is enormously popular with her subjects. She's a familiar sight at important events and is always dressed fashionably. Animals are among her favorite interests, and her pet corgis have their own Facebook

page. She owns and breeds horses, and she often goes to events to watch them race.

People in England, Scotland, Wales, Northern Ireland, and British Commonwealth nations around the world (see box below) seem to be quite happy with "Liz."

WHO'S NEXT IN ENGLAND?

Elizabeth's oldest son, Charles, is next in line to become the British monarch. He's actually been first-in-line since his mother took over in 1952! His son Prince William is next in line after him. William's baby son George would come after his dad.

COUNTRIES THAT ALSO CALL ELIZABETH THEIR QUEEN

The British Commonwealth is an international group of nations that were once colonies or territories of the UK, but now have independent status. However, many of them, like the UK, include the queen as a ceremonial monarch. Here are Commonwealth countries that still honor the Queen:

AUSTRALIA
BAHAMAS
BARBADOS
CANADA
GRENADA
JAMAICA

SAINT KITTS AND NEVIS
SAINT LUCIA
SAINT VINCENT AND THE GRENADINES
SOLOMON ISLANDS
TUVALU

Authors

James Buckley Jr. is the author of more than 125 book for young readers, including more than a dozen titles in the popular *Who Was...?* biography series. He has written many books on sports, including the annual *Scholastic Year in Sports*, as well as on nature, history, social studies, astronauts, dolphins, bugs, antique cars, pirates, and surfing, to name just a few.

He lives in Santa Barbara, California.

Diane Bailey has written 40 non-fiction books for children and teens, on topics ranging from science to sports to celebrities. Diane also works as a freelance editor, helping authors who write novels for children and young adults. Diane has two sons and lives in Kansas with her two dogs.

Picture Credits